The
Boy

The Boy

An Autobiography

Alan G. Mackie

© Alan G. Mackie 2014

All rights reserved. No part of this publication may be reproduced, stored in a retrieval system, or transmitted, in any form or by any means, electronic, mechanical, photocopying, recording or otherwise, without the prior permission of the copyright owner and the publisher.

Published by Mackay Books
144 Bothwell Park Road
R D 2
Waiuku 2682
New Zealand
mackaybooks@live.com

Covers
Original front cover idea by writer and Joseph Marcom
Final back and front covers by Marcus Dela Torre

National Library of New Zealand
ISBN 978-1-927233-08-5

Dedicated to Pinder Mackie
(1917-1966)

Foreword

As his former counsellor and mentor, it was an honour to be asked by Alan Mackie to write a foreword for his biography which he finished only shortly before he died peacefully in his sleep at home in Pauanui, New Zealand, on 26 October 2012.

In this book Alan shares his story about his early childhood experiences in a way that lets readers see what was going on through the eyes of the boy he once was. I found his story so deeply disturbing that the task of writing a foreword seemed a somewhat daunting challenge. When I mentioned this to Alan, tears came to his eyes that let me know he had felt understood without judgement, which was exactly what he wanted his readers to feel from reading his story. It confirmed to me again the power of compassion and validation, which is so essential for survivors of sexual abuse in order to heal and recover from their shameful past.

I first met Alan in 2002 when he came to me for counselling while I worked at a Salvation Army social service agency in Hamilton. He came seeking help to address issues relating to his childhood sexual abuse. Within a safe, trusting and supportive relationship, Alan found the courage to talk about the tragic childhood abuse he had suffered and his struggles through life as a male sexual abuse survivor. It enabled him to gain an understanding of how the sexual abuse had affected him psychologically, emotionally, spiritually and physically from an early age, and how this had disrupted his attachment bonding with his family as well as his development.

In this book he not only describes well how the unquantifiable damage sexual abuse had impacted on him at various levels of his functioning, but also the struggles he faced through his teenage years and into adulthood. The tale of how he survived the really bad abuse of his life makes for inspirational, if incredibly sad, reading. Apart from the therapeutic value to himself in writing his story, it was Alan's wish that this book would benefit others who, like him, were damaged by what happened to them.

It is estimated that approximately one in three boys in New Zealand have been sexually abused before the age of sixteen. In the majority of cases it is by another male. Boys generally don't tell because of guilt, shame and fear of being, and being seen as, gay. Therefore they keep it secret and try to deny that it ever happened. They block out the memories and repress the horrible feelings, 'toughing it out' and hiding behind false masks to hide their guilt, shame and fears. Many turn to drugs and alcohol to sooth and numb out unbearable feelings as a way of coping but while these provide temporary relief, they are mostly destructive and exacerbate problems that lead them to hit a crisis point. Studies show a massive link between male sexual abuse and substance abuse. They also show that 90% of male adolescents who attempt suicide have been sexually abused. Male psychiatric patients are more than twice as likely, than men in the general population, to have been sexually abused.

Alan's story provides a graphic description of how it felt to be a child sexual abuse victim. It successfully illustrates how the damaging effects caused him to experience post trauma symptoms, psychosis and mental health problems. Modern studies have found a strong causal link between sexual abuse and psychosis, which is why sexual abuse victims tend to show up in the mental health system in large numbers.

Like so many other victims, Alan found himself in the public mental health system where staff traditionally focused on treating the symptoms but not the cause. Alan's story illustrates how psychiatry failed to recognise and acknowledge his sexual abuse as the major cause of his confusion, psychosis and schizophrenic-type behaviours, and therefore failed to provide him with appropriate treatment. Specialised trauma recovery counselling is not available in the public mental health system in New Zealand for people affected by sexual violence. Trauma recovery therapy and counselling are not part of psychiatry's vocabulary or method of treatment. Trauma survivors generally receive conventional psychiatric treatment based on the 'medical model' approach involving drugs and nursing care.

People affected by sexual violence are often told they have a mental 'illness', a 'chemical imbalance in the brain' or a 'life-long illness' requiring drugs called 'medication' to keep them stable. Survivors know that their sexual abuse is the cause of the mental 'injury' and often feel misunderstood and misdiagnosed, and then are sedated with psychotropic drugs that have debilitating side affects. While anti-depressants and anti-psychotic drugs can be a useful short-term solution for people in a crisis, it doesn't address the cause. Everyone knows that drugs do not make the effects of sexual abuse trauma disappear.

Alan's story demonstrates how the 'treatment' he was subjected to during his many years in the mental health system was unhelpful, ineffective and counterproductive to his hopes and expectations for healing and recovery. His story tells of how he was heavily over-medicated with powerful drugs that kept him in a state of 'chemical fog' and feeling like a 'zombie' much of the time – impairing his functioning and creating psychosis that tempted him to kill himself to end his confusion. The forced drugging with toxic chemicals known as 'treatment', made Alan's years of incarceration in the mental health system worse than being in prison. It was experienced by him as a case of the system afflicting the already afflicted.

Research has found that the highest rate of suicide in New Zealand is through poisoning, from mental health patients ingesting the 'medications' prescribed by their psychiatrists. Statistics do not include the number of patient deaths caused by poisoning through excessive dosages of drugs administered by psychiatry.

Alan's story is not uncommon - similar stories can be found often in the experiences of many people affected by sexual violence who become patients in the public mental health system. His is only one of the many tragic stories I have heard during my many years as a trauma recovery counsellor.

Alan was fortunate to survive such a system when so many others haven't. As an ex-patient of Lake Alice Hospital, Alan later received a sum of money from the NZ government as compensation for the maltreatment he was subjected to as a child, young person and adult patient in that mental institution. He used the money to buy himself a car.

Alan's story goes on to describe how difficult it was for him to reintegrate into society after his release from hospital. People like him really struggle to survive in this world with little or no support. Searching for ways to get free of his demons, Alan tried to find a purpose, meaning and direction for his life.

A significant turning point came for him when he found a supportive group who influenced his decision to put his faith in Jesus Christ. The changes that followed lead him to recognise that he needed to address issues that related to his past. Counselling enabled him to revisit his childhood, gain new understanding and awareness and grieve the multiple losses of all the innocent little boy had suffered as a result of what had been done to him. It gave him self compassion and an understanding of how he came to become a psychologically damaged victim. It was good to see him progress through the stages of his healing recovery journey and I admired his resilience during this process.

Validation and normalisation of post trauma symptoms and common issues for male sexual abuse survivors helped Alan to reframe the long-held faulty beliefs and to redefine himself as no longer being a 'schizophrenic' but rather as a survivor of childhood sexual abuse deserving of respect, compassion and support. As a result of counselling Alan was able to reclaim his dignity which allowed his essential-self to emerge with new confidence, power and hope for a future, and the freedom to pursue his dreams for a normal life.

He also set himself new goals to study towards a social work qualification. It was his dream to be able to help others in pain, those that needed someone to rescue them from the point of suicide. So he enrolled in a local tertiary institution to study for a qualification in social work. I admired his courage and determination considering that he had very limited formal education. He worked extremely hard and his assignments were always of an exceptionally high standard. After four years of diligent commitment to his studies, he graduated with a Bachelor Degree in Social Work in 2010. This was the fulfilment of his dream, and a great achievement given his life story as described in this book.

It was wonderful to see Alan finally find employment in a local community social service agency as a qualified social worker. This meant a lot to him as it gave him a new identity, status and purpose to life. His past experiences enabled him to have good understanding and awareness of the struggles of those he worked with. Alan became their strong advocate and would go the extra mile to ensure their issues were well resolved. Tributes at his funeral gave testimony to his dedication and commitment to his work as a competent and professional social worker.

From an ex-mental patient to a social worker, Alan's faith in a loving God and the hope this gave him enabled him to change his life in a miraculous way. His story is immensely powerful and is an extraordinary testament to the human desire for survival.

It was Alan's hope that this book will assist other male sexual abuse survivors everywhere to emerge from their shame and isolation into healing and recovery. It is also to educate professionals who work with people affected by sexual violence. To this end Alan Mackie has made an important contribution to this still largely unexposed social problem.

'Share your burdens with one another, and so fulfil the law of Christ' (Galatians 6:2)

Anton Roest (B.Couns.PGDip.Supervision)
Counsellor. NZAC.
Tairua, NZ
antonroest@clear.net.nz

Male Sexual Abuse Sequelae Chart is on my website. Address - antonroest.co.nz.

Warning: This book contains explicit content with detailed descriptions of sexual abuse that may be disturbing to readers. Caution is advised.

Preface

There are many reasons for writing this story, I'm not sure I understand all of them, but I'll list those I am aware of.

Number one was a need to get it out of me and down on paper, an 'externalising' if you will, in all its sordid and graphic detail. I wrestled with that aspect of my writing, but felt that anything less was to short-change and minimise the trauma undergone by victims of childhood sexual, physical and emotional abuse, and in so doing also deny counsellors, therapists and others the depth of insight I can offer.

Part of that externalising process was catharsis, part was a need to record it in some more permanent form than in my memory. The reasons for that are many-fold:

A hope – of generating understanding and through that understanding, a measure of forgiveness from the many people I have hurt;

A wish – that others who have suffered childhood abuse may, to some extent, see themselves in these pages, and in revisiting their own experiences, obtain healing and, if like me, come to accept and forgive themselves for being the damaged people they mostly are, and instead, see themselves as heroic survivors;

Understanding – from friends, families, partners who may gain a window into the tortured souls of the survivors in their lives;

Greater public awareness – accurate figures are difficult to obtain, but it is widely accepted that upwards of 80% of both male psychiatric patients and prison inmates have been victims of childhood sexual abuse;

Human loss – the depth of shame felt especially by male victims, and, therefore, their reluctance to disclose abuse, may go some way to explaining why their suicide numbers are four to five times higher than those for females.

Alan G. Mackie

> *"If you negotiate the minefield in the drive,*
> *Beat the dogs and cheat the cold electronic eyes,*
> *And if you make it past the shotgun in the hall,*
> *Dial the combination, open the priest hole*
> *And if I'm in, I'll tell you what's behind the wall."*
> *The Final Cut* Pink Floyd

1   Sing a Song of Sixpence

The boy's finger traced the outlines and hemmed edges of folded sheet and blanket trapped behind the wire-wove springs of the bunk above him.

His imagination traced hills and valleys of far and distant lands, lands of not here, lands of not now, lands of no fear and no pain. But he did not think in those terms. To do so would destroy the reprieve and crash him back into the now, the fear, the pain.

Too late. The thought had leaked into his consciousness, his hand dropped away from that fast fading landscape and onto his stomach, a stomach that was quickly flooding with the familiar family of leaden sourness and knotted apprehension.

Was that a scraping footfall? His father's unsteady step on the concrete path that ran past The Boy's bedroom window? He held his breath, straining to listen as his heart thumped in his ears, mocking his frozen concentration and denying him his hearing. Slowly, his still-silence eased and he slumped back into the bed as no footfall fell to match the one imagined.

"Wait 'til your father gets home." His memory replayed his mother's words. "Then you'll be for it!"

His mind replayed the implications, his heart replayed the fear, his ear replayed the chilling note of enjoyment in her voice; the sick sour dread once again gripped his stomach, tears threatened as his body pre-played the hiding to come.

It wasn't 'til years later that the dynamics of the situation finally made some sort of sick sense to him. He was accustomed enough to the way the script ran …

His father would be late; his mother would become progressively more annoyed as the evening drew into darkness. Her eyes, through the window above the kitchen bench, searched the long road in vain for her overdue husband, finding instead, in her son, a closer more accessible target for her rising anger.

His father would be drunk, his mother would greet him at the door with some tale of The Boy's misbehaviour. The Boy would be summoned, trembling, to the kitchen to hear of his offences and receive his thrashing, the fists raining down, punctuating his cries of pain and fear as his mother stood observing the execution of sentence, periodically interjecting, "Not the head! Not the head!"

Only later did the concept of a 'whipping boy' filter through to a personal application, and the understanding that his mother's suppressed angry disappointment at having an alcoholic husband and his father's deep shame in being one, both found their relief … in his pain. That pain, however, was physical and had a duration, a start and an end. The much deeper pain knew no temporal bounds; it seemed to reach forward into the eternal as well as stretch back into time before memory. The boy could only imagine an existence without it. How sweet that state would be!

Once, he had done more than imagine. He had tasted the possibility in the form of his older brother's point 22 rifle.

One desperate home-alone day he took it from the wardrobe. He could feel his pulse thumping in his ears, but a strange cold calm wrestled with his fear for ownership of his hands.

He opened the small oiled cardboard ammunition packet nesting the rounds in military rows, selected and loaded a sleek shiny brass shell in the chamber, working the rifle bolt several times, just to hear and feel the smooth precise clicking efficiency of the mechanism. He swung the stock away from himself, tilted the gun, and placed the barrel between his young lips. The steel was cold and tasted of gun oil; the foresight scratched the roof of his mouth as he angled the rifle up toward his oddly cool clear brain, and eased the trigger to first pressure, then off, then first pressure, then off, then first pressure …

He slowly lowered the gun, withdrew it from his mouth, unloaded it, and put everything back exactly in place, all without a conscious thought.

He didn't think about that incident for several days. Just going through the motions had somehow brought release, knowing he had the means to end his life at any time, meant he didn't have to … well, not just yet …

He realised with a cold shock that he was back in the present. He sometimes lost track of where he was in time and space, and as the 'now' rushed back and re-established all its parameters of recent past and imminent future, he lay there, wondering what had brought him to this point in his life, but in permitting that thought, he allowed memories to surface, slowly but unstoppably, from the swamp of his past. Like marsh gas belching up from a pond bed of fetid and decaying matter, long submerged under the weed and weight of time and neglected intentions.

The deep and palpable sadness, through which he viewed both himself and the world he lived in, permeated all and everything. In an effort to shake his mood, he consciously drifted back in his memories, searching for a time when he felt good, well, perhaps that was asking too much. He would settle for a time when he felt not as bad.

An impatient memory, fighting suppression, pushed itself forward into his consciousness; unbidden and demanding it started to play out on the screen of his mind …

The teenage lad from across the road had always seemed to cause a mixture of emotions in The Boy, a shifting, swirling blend of fear and excitement, attraction and repulsion, friend and enemy, which he had never been able to, or perhaps never previously found the courage to, analyse. One lazy day the teen had all too casually drifted over as The Boy was mucking around in the basement. It had a dirt floor and an old, heavy, wooden workbench with a much-prized 6-inch engineer's bench vice proudly bolted at one end. The jaws were scarred with hacksaw cuts, hammer bruises and paint spills from a hundred half-completed projects, the rough concrete walls on either side of the never-cleaned, web-draped window, were hung with various tools. Under the bench lurked drawers, cupboards and boxes of bits and pieces, unidentifiable, priceless treasures, just waiting to be combined and transformed into all manner of marvellous inventions.

The Boy was idly filling in the time after walking home from primary school. His two older brothers were yet to arrive on the bus from high school, his mother was still at her new job, "To bring in some extra money for those little luxuries" and his father was still at work … or in the pub.

Small talk from the teenager quickly drifted into him closing the basement doors, two big awkward wooden bi-fold doors with clumsy extensions to the bottom of them, which had been added to reach down to the lowered ground level where his father had dug out the basement floor and, probably illegally, removed several concrete piles to turn the central area into a garage to accommodate the family car.

"I'll just close the doors 'cause of the draught," the teenger said.

In the dim light from the workbench window, the teenager moved closer to The Boy, stood behind him, placed his hands on The Boy's shoulders, and began to massage them …

Sing a Song of Sixpence
*Sing a song of sixpence,
turn your eye away.
Don't notice as your baby boy,
now finds no fun in play.*

Don't hear his sobbing echo,
down the lonely streets of night.
Don't see the ghosts a'gathering,
don't help him in his fight.

The TV needs updating
and the lounge suite's looking old,
so never mind, as silently,
he slips into the cold.

The light has gone out in his eye,
the laughter from his lip.
A hunted, haunted loneliness,
Has got him in its grip.

He's now the prey of predators,
who struck while you were out.
They own him mind and body now,
you own a 'nicer' house.

So, sing a song of sixpence,
as they hollow out his heart.
You did everything for him,
why'd he fall apart?

Speaking in a soothing yet directive tone, the youth's hands held The Boy close; The Boy was very fit and surprisingly strong. Gymnastics, judo, the ceaseless energy of youth, combined with a mind that wouldn't let him be still, all had honed his young body into muscular perfection. His friend's hands gently moved down over his arms and across onto his chest, caressing and calming, then lower, onto his taut stomach. They softly teased The Boy's shirt loose from his pants and slid underneath it.

The Boy felt a strange wave of nervous excitement, the teenager hovered over his young prey, his hot breath warming his neck as practised hands explored his smooth body, The Boy felt the excitement and fear of the forbidden, and also a sense of power, a strange importance, and flattery, that he, the family outcast, the unplanned and unwanted son, was the focus of attention and attraction from this 'mentor'. This excitement increased as he felt the bulge of the teenager's penis pressing against his butt.

"Remember when we used to do this?" whispered the youth.

The Boy didn't ... didn't ... didn't … then did!

Fear washed over his mind as he realised the implications of that rhythmical motion and the now obvious size and hardness of the pressing bulge.

The youth's hands moved down over The Boy's jeans and massaged him into erection. When they met no resistance, he deftly undid the belt buckle, unbuttoned the fly, and delved smoothly into his underpants, complimenting him on his fine wisp of pubic hair, fondling his balls, and stroking his penis. The Boy, paralysed by fear and excitement, did not stop the youth, and so allowed his jeans to drop to his ankles and his underpants to slide to his knees.

Then something further shocked and thrilled The Boy. The youth glided in front of him and dropped to his knees, cradling his balls, kissing and licking his penis, then opening his mouth and sliding his lips over the knob and down over the shaft of The Boy's cock.

The Boy writhed and twitched with uncontrollable movements as he struggled to adjust to levels of feeling and sensation he had not experienced before, or … he struggled with something. Was it a memory?

The youth, still kneeling in front of him, stroked The Boy's calf, his inner thigh, and then, coating his thumb with saliva, pressed it against and then into The Boy's anus.

"Remember when I used to put my cock right inside you?" the youth asked, in an excited tone.

The Boy's nine short years began rolling backwards, the events of his past presenting themselves one by one, faster and faster, in an avalanche of memories, as puzzle piece after puzzle piece tumbled, crashed and slammed into place. Feelings, thoughts, nightmares, memories, terrors, horrors and strange feelings, and urges that other boys did not share or understand … his awareness of something very alien and wrong deep within his soul. Now, all of this, at last, made sense. His mind spiralled backwards in time …

Hey Little Boy
Hey little boy, little boy so young,
whose mind is pure and free.
How can I warn you? How can I say
to get down off his knee?

You see no darkness in his heart,
no evil in his soul.
The 'kindness' he is showing you,
will soon become control.

His 'friendship' has a purpose,
to win a young boy's trust.
He wants to use your body,
to satisfy his lust …

How can you know the pain to come?
The horrors you will face?
The monsters that will haunt your heart,
allow no hiding place.

You'll come to know the chasms,
of loneliness, despair,
the mental maze of madness,
and desolation's lair.

Unseen chains and leaden shoes,

will weigh your fettered feet,
your days will be as dark as night,
and emptiness your meat.

Hey little boy, little boy so young,
little boy of only three,
I wish I could shout down the years,
hey little boy! ... little boy! ... flee!

The youth felt the sudden change of atmosphere in the basement, there had been a shift in the world, he sensed it, and became concerned.

The Boy stood fixed, frozen, trembling, his body was there, present, but his mind was in another time and place, a long ago place, a place of fear and warm grass and panic and pain and blood and macrocarpa hedges, and ...

"Don't tell on me and I won't tell on you, ok? Ok?" the youth said, rising to his feet, fear in his voice as he watched The Boy's vacant eyes lose their distant fixed glaze and snap back to the present.

Both hurriedly adjusted their clothing. Frightened, embarrassed and confused, with mind whirling, spinning, The Boy fumbled open the garage door and emerged into the relative safety of the afternoon light, feeling as if he had just walked out of a dark movie theatre and needed to reorient himself in this time and this place, out of a movie that was intended for an audience a lot older than he.

He understood in that moment, that years before something had happened, something profound, a dark and evil element had entered his life and his heart, no not his heart, his mind, no not that either. It had entered the spaces in between; he struggled with the concept of a spirit, but that was where it was. It lived alongside his personality, sharing the same internal space, he had dimly sensed it, it had been there, drifting just outside of his awareness. Now he felt it, he knew it and it knew him. Now, whatever it was had just reawakened, just grown stronger, stretched, extended and wrapped its black tentacles tighter.

2   It's Starting to Make Sense

In the following days, the events of that afternoon were to play over and over in his troubled mind. So many questions had been answered by the older youth's reference to previous sexual experiences. Things that had been distant, puzzling, fuzzy memories. All out of focus. Until now. He now understood the agitation, which sometimes gripped and confused him, agitation as he climbed the steps to the footbridge, which arched over the local railway track. The strong aversion that he had to using a shortcut alongside that same track. The odd 'driven' necessity he felt to search for blood in his underpants whenever he removed them.

It also left him feeling even more separate, more alone, and more isolated than ever.

The teenager was not to know of the rift which existed between The Boy and his family, a rift of very long standing, a rift which never closed, only widened, a rift which made him the perfect victim. The teenager also need not have worried about being told on; he was the closest person in The Boy's life. The earlier abuse had worked its effect, driving a wedge of shame and difference between The Boy and all others.

He did not know why he had never felt a bond between himself and his family; only knew the occasions when the tenuous relationship chilled and widened. The most hurtful of those was one Christmas holiday when his two brothers, one four years older, the other six, were off on their own adventures, either with friends or a school camp, he was not sure now. Anyway, he was on holiday alone with his parents. All trips away in the family car had now become a pub-crawl. His father did not drive, never had.

The family car was a deep olive green 1936 Ford De Soto, a huge tank of a vehicle, with running boards, and a spare wheel mounted proudly beside the bird wing bonnet, the headlights raised on stalks staring fixedly forward. It had a little crank handle on the dashboard to wind out the windscreen, which was hinged at the top and so ventilated the interior on hot Central Otago holidays.

The enormous rear bench seat folded down to allow access to the copious rear trunk. It should also have boasted a valve radio and a long telescopic aerial. This radio was sadly missing when the family had gone to pick up their purchase, a cause of much disappointment among them and an absence their father chose not to press. He reserved his assertiveness for other things. The duty of driving the behemoth was left to his mother.

Such was the spaciousness of the interior that one Saturday when the local rugby ground was deemed too wet to play on and another venue chosen, the entire young boys' team put their uniforms and boots in the tin trunk, which was permanently strapped on to the rear carrier, piled into the car and were transported en masse to the new ground.

The Boy was not sure, but presumed his mother's chauffeuring was due to a general lack in his father's physical co-ordination; he displayed a poor ability to operate even hand tools. He had once produced three discarded attempts at constructing a simple letterbox, and the family was left with the fourth attempt, a mismatched oddity, which nevertheless served its intended function. Whatever the reason, this car-driving arrangement left his father free to drink.

Consequently, trips in the car took twice or twenty times as long as they should have. Each country pub, and they were many in those days, became another stop in a tortuous trek. His mother would motor quietly along, but as if endowed with a sixth sense, his father would stir from his drunken dosing as they approached a pub, and quietly command that they "Just call in for a minute or two," each 'minute or two' inevitably turning into The Boy sitting in the car park, sometimes bribed with a raspberry and lemonade drink, waiting for the eventual reluctant emergence of a progressively more drunken father.

All this culminated one afternoon in a camping ground when, after yet another alcohol fuelled row, The Boy's father eventually stormed off saying, "That's it, I'm gone, you can have the kids, you can have the house, everything", The Boy pleading with him not to go, father saying he'll visit, then walking off, The Boy's mother sending him to beg his father to turn around.

The Boy did not know how far he went following behind his father, now walking, now running, to catch his father's long strides, The Boy's face floured with the dust of the country road and streaked with tears as he pleaded with him not to leave. Eventually, his father stopped, paused a time, then turned, and began the long walk back to the camping ground and a tenuous reconciliation. This event, troubling as it was, was not the worst of it.

The incident was never mentioned, and festered in his young mind. It inevitably had to find expression, and he blurted it all out one evening to his two elder brothers who had demanded to know why, even under threat, he would not stop his bedtime sobbing.

The following day, after they had sought answers from the parents, he was summoned to the bedroom where the family was in discussion. His parents stood shoulder to shoulder beside his two brothers.

His mother looked him right in the eye and said "What's this story you've concocted? You must have imagined it all; that never happened!"

He felt the stab of betrayal in his heart, and again felt the blackness within, stretch, extend and wrap its tentacles tighter.

From that point on, The Boy knew he could never rely or depend on support from any member of his family. He was alone, his outcast status confirmed, sealed. The event wounded him terribly, and whether it was that, or his recent re-seduction by the neighbour, or both, he didn't know, but at age nine, The Boy started to wet his bed. It was also at age nine that his school became sufficiently concerned at the change in his demeanour and his poor performance that they employed an Education Department psychologist to assess him.

He noted The Boy's intelligence, his loneliness, his distractibility, and his poor ability around numbers and spelling. It was a strange form of numerical dyslexia, no, that did not quite capture it. It seemed to drift over into a poor memory for shapes and the meanings of shapes; peoples' faces, for instance, took quite a number of meetings to become part of his visual library.

His parents had insisted he learn a musical instrument and chose the ukulele; this was a type of sustained torture to a boy who simply lacked the gift. In time he guessed he could have mastered a tune or two, but knew it would sound like he was 'playing by numbers', because he would have been. Thankfully, the ukulele venture came to an abrupt end when his mother, in a fit of rage, broke it over him.

A related area was his inability to translate exactly what the hands of a clock were saying. He could tell the time in a mute form, he 'knew what the time was', but to bring that from an inner knowledge and put it into the language of 'twenty to seven' or 'nine forty five' was mostly beyond him. This caused immense frustration for his parents, and once, when he was again late home from his wanderings, he was made to stand in the kitchen, staring at the clock, until he told them the time, an impossible task for his scrambled thinking. He stood there for over two hours; he knew two hours had passed because the minute hand had twice swept the full face of the clock. He watched as the hand again began to tick and tock its way tirelessly and impassively around the dial. But he was simply unable to translate their position into language, and was sent off to bed by his disgusted father with "idiot!" and "nincompoop" ringing in his ears and stinging his heart.

The psychologist left guidance notes for dealing with the 'superior and gifted' child. But what carried more weight with him than this report, was the School Principal announcing to him, "You will never amount to anything".

His personality quirks and oddities only served to distance him even further from his family. The Boy was later to compare the relationship between himself, his parents, and his two older brothers, to the digits on his hand.

They, represented by all four fingers, standing side by side in matched unison, and he, like the thumb, a distant, mismatched and awkward addition, a ready target for and an explanation of any family dysfunction.

The Boy didn't know why, but he never felt close to his mother. Perhaps it was the cumulative trauma of many early childhood illnesses, or perhaps the events he was later told of, where, for instance, during one of his parent's frequent parties, his mother found him still and blue, and lifting him limp from the cot, discovered his nappies soaked in blood, the result of a bleed from a poorly completed circumcision.

The Boy saw himself as a ready target for and an explanation of any family dysfunction.

Or the occasion when she dropped him between the platform and the carriage of the halted passenger steam train, necessitating the careful advancing of the train until he could be lifted from the tracks.

Or maybe the fact that his very existence was not intended, that when it was realised he was indeed on the way, he failed his parents by being yet another boy, a point which his mother made clear to him on many occasions, and far from telling The Boy that he was wanted, loved and valued, frequently told him instead, "I hate you, I wish you'd never been born!"

His father took a different tack. An attitude of disdain, of open disapproval. No, on second thoughts, disapproval was too active a word. That implied more emotional interaction than he experienced. What his father showed was more of an indifference, seldom speaking directly to him. In fact, he referred to him in the third person as 'the boy' or 'the idiot' or 'the nincompoop'. What he emanated toward The Boy was a sort of deep disappointment, or perhaps the attitude one might display toward an annoying stray cat or dog that one felt a grudging obligation to feed and water.

His father never talked to him except to impart necessary information or commands. The Boy had no memory of ever having had a conversation with his father. The predominant feeling toward him was one of fear, of someone to be avoided, as much to avoid the emotional pain of rejection as to avoid the physical pain of the frequent beatings. He had stopped trying to 'be good'. He didn't know what that meant anymore.

The hidings came no matter what he did. They served the needs of the adult world, not his. As a result of his sexual violation, there was a trampling of his personal boundaries, his sense of where he began and ended, of what was personal and private to him and where other people's space started and stopped. Along with that, his ability to understand, feel and, therefore, to behave within the social norms had been extinguished. He lived within a different reality to his peers, so even his parents' frequent threats to disown him, have him committed to Cherry Farm, the local psychiatric hospital, or consign him to borstal, were just more slings and arrows from the world of adults.

The natural link between actions and consequences, things he did or did not do, and the resultant rewards or punishments he received, had ceased to figure in his reasoning. In fact, they made no sense to him anymore. They were tied more to the volatile moods of his mother and intermittent sobriety of his father than to anything he did. This breakdown of a knowable, logical and predictable world spread from his home life to his school, and indeed to all interactions with adults. As a result of his internal chaos, he soon achieved the highest record for earning detentions from his female teachers and the strap from his male teachers.

Over time, The Boy retreated further and further from adults. They now all just represented hurt, pain and betrayal. It was safer to be alone.

During his darker times of aloneness, The Boy thought that maybe he was adopted. That all would be explained when his real father and real mother dramatically appeared to whisk him away to a life of love and peace and warmth, a life of being wanted and loved. The Boy had some reason to think that perhaps he was not his father's son. He didn't look anything like his father. His father was quite tall whereas he quite short; his father quite slim, he rather stocky; his father dark haired, he a redhead.

Then there were the times when he and his brothers had lain in bed hearing their parents argue about sex – well, mostly their mother complaining about their father's lack of interest in her, which only fuelled his doubts about his parentage.

There was also that day when he had gone into his parents' bedroom when, as usual, he was home first and alone in the house. He had explored his mother's wardrobe and discovered a cache of pornographic novels amongst his mother's things. It shocked him at the time, as she was to all outward appearances a very proper and virtuous woman, not at all attracted by such carnal and sensuous matters. In fact, she had pounced upon her eldest son's rumoured interest in such areas as wholly distasteful. He had dared to express an interest in a girl at his rugby club, and, in fact, had been seen kissing her! This resulted in him being roundly chastised and shamed at the evening meal table.

The strange dichotomy in his mother's thinking – sex is repulsive and attractive, evil and good – was not unknown to him but in a very different context, which was even now playing out in his mind, first occasionally, then each day, then more and more often until it occupied much of his thoughts. The terrible sexual secrets he shared with his neighbour frightened and excited him, and drew him, subtly but irresistibly. He felt like a green leaf plucked loose from an overhanging tree, fluttering down into a languid country stream, to find itself gliding on a ride to an unknown end. Slowly, casually at first, then pitching and bucking over rippling rapids, gaining speed, now drifting into a wider gentler part of the river, now being held in the outermost orbit of a slowly spiralling whirlpool, irretrievably caught in its circular current, partly wanting to break free from this strange pull, mostly knowing it couldn't, caught, spinning, in a web of water being drawn ever inward. Deep within him, a black tentacle twitched, a hooded eye half opened then lazily closed, and he knew he would go back to his seducer.

3 ... Said the Spider to the Fly

The Boy was perceptive. As a child he was very quick to pick up on non-verbal cues and read the moods of others. With a physically violent father and an emotionally unstable mother, it had become a necessary survival skill. Because of the estrangement and lack of love he experienced from his family, he had become eager to please others, in return for acceptance and approval; in fact it was now a constant ache.

Since his re-acquaintance with his seducer, he had trawled his memories. He wanted to fill in the gaps in the jigsaw puzzle of his earlier years. After questioning the teenager, the youth explained that he had 'helpfully' offered to escort The Boy home from the local kindergarten for his over-stretched mother. The youth and his victim revisited the kindergarten ... they leaned over the closed gate, The Boy pointing out familiar features, the sandpit, the jungle gym, the monkey bars, the roundabout, and as his eyes fell upon the see saw he remembered a pretty little straw haired girl, his first crush, he could even remember her name. He and this girl would spend all their playtimes together. The see-saw had been her favourite. He remembered nap time, lying beside her, lost in her eyes.

How different things might have been.

They turned slowly away, leaning against the fence, their elbows resting on the wooden rail, and both looking up the incline toward the footbridge, which arched over the railway track.

"Well, shall we start back?" the youth asked. Without further words they started walking.

As they approached the footbridge, The Boy again felt the familiar rising apprehension, the light-headedness verging on nausea, but this time he knew why. This had been the turning point in the walk home from the kindergarten. Over the footbridge and straight ahead meant staying on the public road and safety. Taking the shortcut alongside the railway track meant otherwise. They took the shortcut.

The path was not overgrown as he had imagined it would be; obviously it was used by some of the locals. He had avoided it, again because of that odd apprehension, which, until recently, he hadn't begun to understand. As they walked the track, the youth in front, stick in hand, carefully pushed aside some blackberry vines, then with a "Let's take a look", he had a quick glance around, then ducked off to the side and pushed under a large macrocarpa hedge. It opened out to an area of low flattened grass about two yards across.

"This is where we used to do it," he said, sitting down and motioning The Boy to sit beside him. "This is where I used to fuck you, remember now?" The Boy did, vaguely.

The youth lay back, undid his shirt, exposing an expanse of broad hairless chest and taut abdomen. He kneaded, and then unbuttoned his bulging fly. A huge penis burst out. He reached over and took hold of The Boy's hand, then, enclosing The Boy's hand in his own, began masturbating.

"That's it," he said, "tighter! ... harder! ... faster!"

The Boy obeyed the commands and continued, faster and faster, fascinated by the spectacle before him and the effect he was having on his mentor. A strange excited gurgle escaped from the teemager's throat. The Boy watched in awe as jets of semen erupted and trailed over the smooth olive chest and stomach. His friend moaned, shuddered, relaxed, and his expression moved from ecstasy into a quiet, fulfilled, calm satisfaction, a look of warmth and gratitude sweeping over his face. As he gazed on the giver of this pleasure, The Boy felt a surge of power, of warm belonging, of acceptance, of worth. He felt he was finally of value to someone, he felt. .. yes that was it, he felt loved!

"O.K. Now it's your turn," the youth said.

The older lad peeled open The Boy's clothes and mouthed his penis.

"This time, I want you to root me. I can't do it to you any more, my cock is too big."

He undressed, instructing The Boy to do the same, then he lay face down on the grass.

"Come on, do it, you'll love it!"

The Boy nervously positioned himself on top of the teenager. "Give me your hand," the youth said, and spat a gob of saliva into it. "Put that on your cock."

The Boy did so and then with his mind roiling with lust and guilt, excitement and fear, pressed his penis between the youths butt cheeks. He pressed against, then after several apologetic adjustments, suddenly penetrated his friend.

He gasped as sensations which he had never before experienced, coursed through his young body. This was better than anything he had ever felt! The Boy lay full length on his mentor's warm smooth olive body and thrust his penis deep inside him. His sexual excitement grew with every stroke, his pleasure clearly shared by the youth who had again begun moaning, encouraging and praising The Boy's now convulsive thrustings. The Boy had never imagined such sensations were possible. They grew and expanded until they consumed his world and were all that existed. Then, with a tingling rush that began deep in his groin and rapidly flooded through his whole body, he experienced the all-consuming sensual explosion of orgasm. The teenager was right, he did love it! He collapsed in satisfied exhaustion, barely able to process what had just happened.

Over the following days and weeks, that experience and the experiences which were to follow, built upon the foundation of his earlier encounters. And in a case of classic conditioning, what began to be locked into his pubescent mind and associated with sexual pleasure, was the male musk, the smell of his friend's shiny black nest of pubic hair, the wonder of semen and the broad expanse of that smooth muscular olive chest and back. This perverted, subversion of love was to become his understanding of and his substitute for the love, which was otherwise absent in his young life.

4 Little Boys are Cheap Today

Life continued intractably down the road that it was now firmly set upon. In the months following his encounters, his thoughts became increasingly filled with lust. He began to look at other boys and wonder what it would be like to have sex with them. These thoughts were always accompanied by an equal measure of guilt and shame, a huge fear of their exposing and rejecting him if they knew what he was thinking and an ever increasing self loathing.

The darkness in his soul was growing, carrying with it a weight of sadness, a weight that cowed his young shoulders and cast down his eyes, a darkness that threw a shadow over all things present and future, draining the colour out of life and the life out of living. Sex had become a drug that he needed more and more of, but a drug that delivered a decreasing return of enjoyment. What gave him some reprieve from this self condemnation was the approval he received from his abuser. The teenager knew this weakness and began passing The Boy around to a wider and wider circle of older boys. It was as if he were branded, his availability announced, he could not seem to resist their approaches and indeed yearned for their approval, but in the law of diminishing returns he sank deeper and deeper into despair. The Boy saw no escape.

Little Boys are Cheap Today
Dropped off … "This is him."
A lifted eyebrow, a knowing smile,
a nod, a wink, a tilt of the head.
a glance held, a fingertip between the lips.
An arrangement understood.

A few swigs of beer, a few slugs of whiskey,
a cigarette packet slid in the pocket,
a backroom, a garden shed, a cellar,
a no one's home lounge, a hay barn.
Tongue in mouth, fumbled clothes.

Straw in hair, grass seed in socks,
body smells, pubic hairs, walk home,
blood in underpants, semen stains.
Eyes down, pain, tears flowing, shame.
Little boys are cheap today.

It didn't always go 'their' way. One New Year's Eve he was at the house of an older boy who had planned, together with his even older friend, to have The Boy sleep over. He knew them both from YMCA, where the older of the two was a leader; he had come to expect overtures from the leaders in the organisations he had joined.

Sea Cadets was no exception. He half knew what was coming when the group had a weekend sleepover at the clubrooms. He was drifting off to sleep when he felt a hand slyly slipping into his sleeping bag and searching out his. The hand belonged to the group leader, conveniently positioned beside him. It drew The Boy's hand out of his sleeping bag and down into his own, wrapped The Boy's fingers around his already erect penis and began stroking. Swapping hands, the leader reinserted his own back down toward The Boy's sleep-warmed crotch and, freeing his penis, began to masturbate him. The Boy could have extracted both hands and rebuffed the advance, but decided it was easier to comply. It was always easier to comply.

The leader was later reported by another boy whom he also molested. An internal enquiry was held, chaired by the perpetrator's father, who was the most senior member of the Sea Cadet branch. The boys, who disclosed molestation, were asked by him if they had enjoyed it and had encouraged the attention. They were collectively shamed within the group and their names circulated among all the parents.

Just as well I had said nothing, The Boy thought. He left Sea Cadets; his parents never asked him why.

YMCA with its judo, gymnastics and weightlifting, was an irresistible attraction to The Boy. The weightlifting gym was not one he was allowed to be part of, as membership was restricted to those sixteen years and older, but with a coy smile and a flirtatious glance, doors would open.

So after judo and gymnastics on a Saturday morning, he would quietly wander down to the weights room in the basement and work out. Mostly he picked a time when he would be alone. The place smelled of dusty horse hair mats, liniment and stale sweat. He was reluctant to turn the lights on and reveal his presence, but the natural light was poor, the whole building constructed on a steeply sloping section, the concrete foundation walls substantial, the windows small, dirty and few, all covered with metal mesh and cobwebs.

The equipment was mostly old but well serviced and entirely functional. The boy followed the routines set out on yellowed and peeling posters on the walls, with their line drawings of very serious post-Edwardian men with handlebar moustaches, grandpa vests and knickerbockers, dourly illustrating the proper and correct method of exercising. Over time and with diligent increments, The Boy, at the age of twelve, was able to bench press three hundred pounds, a feat not often believed by those he told, but that didn't matter, he knew he could.

He enjoyed the art of judo and progressed steadily through the various gradings, becoming sufficiently proficient that the instructor could use him to demonstrate any new moves and throws to the class. After another successful grading, he was taken aside by the visiting examiner, who, together with the resident instructor, suggested that he had potential and should move on to private tuition. As their talk continued they made quiet but clear mention, that in order to advance further, The Boy needed to more deeply acknowledge the small carved deity always in place at the end of the dojo, and to which the practitioners bowed as they entered and left the dojo or stepped onto or off the mat. Even at this age he was aware of the power of the spiritual realm, and resisted that request as a step he was not prepared to take and soon withdrew from the class.

He continued, however with the gymnastics, and was selected to join the display squad. They toured the lower South Island, putting on demonstrations at Agricultural and Pastoral shows in many country towns. He never found out who, but someone in authority clearly had suspect tastes, as the boys' gymnastics costume was a pair of tight briefs made from black elastic fabric, no socks, no shoes, no singlet, no shorts, just a pair of tight black briefs.

It was from this culture that the two older YMCA boys came, and when they invited him to one of their houses, he knew the subtext, he knew even more the looks they had been giving him.

The parents were away and the two older boys had him call his mother and ask permission for him to stay overnight. She readily agreed. They ate, smoked and drank well into the night, the two not knowing how to broach the real reason for their generosity, The Boy knowing full well where the evening was leading, but deliberately not picking up on their cues, nor making it easy for them as they exchanged knowing but nervous glances. He became progressively drunker and they relaxed a little, imagining an easy seduction and the sex to follow.

After midnight and a final toast to the New Year, the three, wearing only their underpants, climbed into the parents' large bed, he in the middle, still playing dumb, pretending in the dim light not to notice their erections. He could feel the tension as the two older boys wondered how to make the first move and finally reveal their true intent. He had already decided what he was going to allow. But as the lights went out and he lay back, all the alcohol from the nights drinking hit him, and nausea flooded in.

"I'm going to be sick!" he said, as he scrambled from the bed, barely making it to the door of the toilet before throwing up.

As they cleaned up, he got back in bed and feigned sleep until sleep overtook him. In the morning he walked home, smiling to himself that he had eaten their food, smoked their cigarettes, drunk their booze and for once not paid with his body.

He had begun trying to seduce boys his own age, spotting the vulnerable ones just as easily as the older boys spotted him. His victims were the stragglers at the back of the herd, the wounded ones who trailed behind the pack, a slightly needy air about them, the ones like him, starved of adult male approval, easy pickings. He became progressively more selfish and callous in satisfying his own desires, putting his desires before the damage he knew he was doing.

He had discovered a huge rush of pleasure in any fresh conquest he achieved, but this high was fleeting, always followed by a deep guilt at spreading the contagion which he felt his life had become.

The tables were turned one day when a neighbourhood girl, a couple of years older than he, invited him into her otherwise empty house. She put a record on the turntable and opened her parents' liquor cabinet. He smiled at the irony as the song *No Milk Today* filled the house, and, although not yet a teenager, he was accustomed to hard liquor and began slugging straight scotch. Several mouthfuls of scotch and a couple of records later they began kissing and exploring each others' bodies, he with his hand on her breast and she with her hand down his pants.

As their passion progressed she said, "We can't do it here, someone might come home."

He wrapped the scotch in his jersey and followed her out the door and down the road to an empty property at the end of the street. They walked into the light scrub and lay down within a grassed enclosure of broom bushes. He took another swig of scotch and began to caress and kiss her breasts, *well developed for a fourteen year old,* he thought, *and oh so incredibly soft and smooth!*

She was wasting no time in encouraging his erection. To avoid being seen, they rose only to their knees before stripping off their clothes. She produced a condom and rolled it onto his cock and lay back in the warm grass. He moved on top of her, and, with her guidance, entered her warm, moist mound. He began thrusting deep into her, lost in the smell of talcum powder and light perfume, her soft lips, the delicious collision of pubic bones, her vulva clutching at his shaft. His head began to swim from the alcohol, he faltered, felt a wave of nausea, and his penis began to loose its firmness. She noticed and asked what was wrong. He told her in a panting slightly slurred voice that he was going soft from the scotch. Not wanting to lose the condom, she pushed him off her in frustrated disgust, dressed herself, and left him there to finish the bottle and sit in self pity and condemnation over her rejection.

Why did he always screw things up? Such events carried a crushing emotional weight for The Boy. Sitting there in his deepening despair, he once more pondered escaping this life; he sensed the blackness within shuffle a little, spread a little wider, settle and smile as its ownership grew.

5 Boys of a Certain Nature

The police car pulled up in front of The Boy's house and two constables got out. They walked slowly up to the house in that policeman's way and knocked on the door. The Boy sat in silent panic, furiously trying to think which one of the many things he had done would have caused this visit and how much trouble he was going to be in. He couldn't escape; the officers had come to the seldom used front door right alongside his bedroom. They were greeted and ushered down the hall, his mother flicking a withering stare through his bedroom door, but from the relatively light-hearted tone of voices coming from the kitchen he guessed it wasn't too bad.

Apparently they had come to oversee the disassembling of the latest of his risk taking ventures. At the top rear of their long, quarter acre, sloping section was a line of several pine trees, the tallest being just over 100 feet. Using rope obtained by his father from his job on the wharves, The Boy had scaled the tree and fastened one end of it half way up, the other end was tied to another lower tree about 15 yards away. An additional length of lighter rope with a strong stick as a seat was suspended from the middle of the span.

With two boys standing on the bank at the lower end of the span and both swinging the heavy rope, the passenger on the seat could, after sufficient effort and accumulated momentum, be made to perform a complete loop with dizzying and violent force. Occasionally, an unfortunate boy would be dislodged, causing him to fall with a sickening thud. The police were there in response to complaints from neighbourhood parents concerned about the safety of their children.

These sorts of activities took up more and more of The Boy's time; the more dangerous the adventure the better. He had been gifted with an exceptional strength and gymnastic ability, and found such tricks as walking on his hands easy, to the point where he could complete two laps of the school tennis court at the trot on his hands.

One day, a teacher had caught him larking about in the locker room and demanded he drop to the floor and do press ups to burn off energy. When The Boy asked how many, the teacher replied, "Just start counting, I'll tell you when to stop."

The Boy dropped to the floor and began to execute textbook press-ups with his board-rigid body touching the polished floorboards, chin, chest and groin in unison. The teacher eventually walked off down the corridor shaking his head in disbelief as the count rose past fifty.

A friend's father was a mechanic, and under persistent pressure, put together a unicycle from some bike parts. The Boy mastered this in a week, and, bored, soon had the mechanic constructing one with a chain from the pedals down to the wheel. It stood higher than him, which required it to be leaned against a lamppost to mount. He once rode it from his grandparents' house in Mosgiel to his home in Abbotsford, a distance of some 10 miles over the Taieri Ranges. These feats challenged him, gave him a measure of pride, gaining him the approval he craved, but it was short lived and he soon sank back into his steady state of depression, although he would not have recognised it as such. He saw this state as his deserved place and his lot in life.

What began to draw him more and more strongly, were acts which involved personal danger. He took pleasure in walking the wooden handrail, which ran from the local railway station, up the sloping foot ramp, to high above the train tracks. Especially pleasing was timing it so that the billowing smoke and steam from a train enveloped him from underneath as he balanced on top, only his skill standing between him and serious injury or death. This escapade earned him another visit from the police.

The train tracks, which ran through the edge of town, became for him a source of personal testing and therefore escape. He would set out early Saturday morning and walk the line towards the Wingatui tunnel. Halfway there, the line soared above a stream. This feature was known locally as the viaduct and held an awe about it.

Fewer and fewer boys spent time with the lad, some left perhaps because he had hinted at his sexual feelings. Others were not allowed to associate with him because their parents were disturbed by his behaviours and his reluctance to engage with them. Some boys, however, overcame their caution around his growing strangeness and joined him to a degree, if only to serve as witnesses to his increasingly frightening acts, such as balancing on the steel girders of the viaduct, a fall from which would have been fatal.

One of his favourite tricks was to hide under the train tracks as they arched over the viaduct, close his eyes and put his head up at the last second, as the steam train thundered overhead, showering his face in dust and sparks. None would join him in that and only watched in fascinated horror from the embankment.

The Boy looked forward to weekends and would be up quite early on Saturday morning, two whole days stretching out before him as a sweet reprieve. He could set out on another adventure and escape his regular life, if only for a matter of hours. He had studied the timetables of the steam trains plying the route between Dunedin and Mosgiel. Things were reasonably regular during the week, as the trains were a standard form of transport and an alternative to the buses. Come the weekend, however, they became wildly unpredictable as trains were added, depending on race days at the Wingatui horse racing track, or trips to Central Otago for A&P shows, ice skating at Manaburn dam, or even special trains laid on for important rugby matches.

Then, of course, there were the goods trains, which varied depending on coal requirements and stock sales and which ships were in port. So his carefully acquired timetables were, for his purposes, fairly meaningless.

His original intention had been to walk from his home in Abbottsford along the railway track to Wingatui and back. This meant walking through the railway tunnel. It was not very long, maybe one hundred and fifty yards, and, from past excursions, knew that as he entered the mouth and the light behind steadily faded, his eyes would adjust as the glimmer from the opening at the other end steadily grew. He had, in the past, never managed to convince his friends to venture more than fifty yards or so, before their rising fears outweighed their boyish bravado and they turned back towards the entrance. The tunnel continued to both draw and challenge him, its open throat mocking him each time he passed it by on his way to other adventures.

His first plan had been to walk the tunnel to Wingatui and back, timing his passage between trains, but they were so frequent that he found no daylight period could be guaranteed train-free. Consequently, his friends would not join him, so his thinking shifted to just doing it and taking his chances. As the day of his adventure approached, his thinking shifted again, to actively planning on being in the tunnel with a train. As he adjusted to that level of excitement, he decided to go all the way and do his best to be in the tunnel when two trains were passing. He smiled to himself as he suspected that somewhere, deep down, that was what he had hoped for from the start.

Now that would be an adventure.

His chosen day arrived. He told no one, as to do so would virtually guarantee someone telling. More than one of his friends had moved from admiration for his daredevil acts to feeling he had to be protected from himself. Perhaps they were right. On a level of motivation he was yet to confront, these acts lay somewhere between a need to prove his masculinity if only to himself and his desire to die a hero.

He had asked around about the meaning of the various lights and signals along the tracks, but got such a wide variety of answers he knew no one answer could be relied upon, and he didn't want to ask too many questions and arouse suspicion.

He set off and arrived at the tunnel entrance. He had already been passed by a few trains on his journey, so figured his chances were good. His young ears could pick up a train at a fair distance, and he found the age old trick of placing an ear on the rail added a good half mile to his radar. As he arrived at the brick-lined arch, he took a good look around and thought if he did get killed it might take a long time to find his body because the train driver would certainly feel nothing.

He stepped into the tunnel mouth and the rough stones rattled under his feet and echoed off the brick and concrete walls. He had noticed on other incursions that there were periodic alcoves set into the walls of the tunnel to allow a safe bolthole for workmen to shelter in as a train passed. He had decided not to use these as his intention was to lay down in-between the two tracks and allow the trains to pass either side of him. He noticed the temperature drop from the warmth of outside. The rattling of the stones under his feet got louder as the noise of the cicadas faded with the light and his increasing distance from the mouth. There was always a breeze flowing one way or the other through the tunnel. Today it was flowing from the Wingatui end and so had cooled on its underground trip. He told himself this was the reason for his slight shiver as he strode stoically onward.

    He had gotten perhaps sixty yards into the tunnel when he thought he heard it or felt it, a change in the air from the Abbottsford end. Yes. The ever-so-faint rattling roar as an approaching train passed over the hollow amplifier of the concrete viaduct.

    Hardly had that sound confirmed itself in his mind as a train, when it was answered from the Eastern end by the toot of another as it heaved itself into motion from its stop at the Wingatui Station. His shiver transformed into a tremor as the reality of his situation hit home. Now, should he go forward, stay where he was, or chicken out? He figured he had enough time to run back to the entrance and duck into the thick bush at the side of the track; no one would be witness to his failure, no one would know ... no one but him. He pressed on, staying in the middle between the two sets of rails, walking mostly to occupy his thoughts. His deliberate steps became progressively more mechanical and stilted until the rising stress and tension stopped him dead.

He turned, sank to his knees and faced the western entrance. The second train tooted behind him, signalling a tunnel as it approached from Wingatui. By his calculations, the train from Abbottsford, travelling at full speed, would reach him before the closer but slower eastern train. As he thought this, it let out its whoop of a whistle, alerting its passengers to the tunnel ahead.

He lay down flat on the cold sharp stones. He had to hide his face both from the stones and sparks, and from the steam train's headlamp. There would be hell to pay if he was caught pulling a stunt like this one. He flipped up his collar and cupped his hands over his ears as the train, tooting in full furious flight, raged into the tunnel mouth. The noise was horrendous – a hundred armoured horses on a metal road would not compete. The floor of the tunnel shook, and, as the roaring crashing noise, the rushing wind, the snorting squirting steam, the hot cinders and hailstorm of small stinging stones reached its climax, it was suddenly doubled with the arrival of the eastbound train.

The combined events had an unexpected element; the sheer violence had a disorienting effect. He no longer had any sure sense of where he was in relation to up, down or sideways. He was so buffeted by the volume of noise and the competing bow waves, he had to work very hard to relax, concentrate on lying still and fight the urge to 'correct' his orientation. He quickly pulled his tee shirt over his mouth and breathed through it as the trapped smoke from the two trains filled every space and threw him into an eye-streaming coughing fit.

The trains passed, the dust and stones settled, the air grew calm, the noise retreated, and the smoke cleared with the gentle breeze. He lay there wondering if it had really happened. The Boy rolled onto his back and roared with laughter. He had thought it would be an adventure ... it was ... it sure was.

The power and weight of a steam train had other applications considerably less dangerous. One of these was to flatten pennies. This required knowledge of the train timetable, or, more commonly for The Boy, a good ear, quick actions and a steady nerve. A train, decelerating into a station or pulling slowly out, lacked the momentum to produce a prizewinning disc; the best results were obtained from a train in full flight.

The penny was placed carefully on the track with the thickest edge toward the oncoming train, a good gob of spit to stop it jiggling off the rail from the mounting vibrations. He then retreated to the side as the train thundered past, often to the blast of a steam whistle as the annoyed engine drivers once again had to shoo the red haired lad from their path. Fierce competition was engaged in to see how much could be added to the one and a quarter inch diameter of the hapless coins, which were displayed with great pride in the school playground like holy relics. Any prize pennies, flung aside by the speeding train and lost in the long grass beside the railway tracks, were deeply missed.

Other pursuits were a little less life threatening and involved carrying sheets of corrugated iron, stolen from railway huts, deep into the pine forest, where one end of the sheet was crudely beaten with rocks up into a curve and the whole fashioned into a sled with rough vine reins. A course down the hill between trees was carefully chosen, marked out, and formed with banked up earth and pine needles. Frightening speeds were attained on the bed of dry pine needles down tree-studded slopes, and many a gashed and bruised body had to be explained to parents, but displayed with a feigned casualness at Monday morning school.

Some of his escape days in the bush were solitary; he took his frogging net and tin. Stripping naked, he would slip into the chilly ponds, submerging himself up to his chin, and creep slowly toward his quarry, croaking expertly, and, as the big green and brown dappled bull frogs responded to this territorial challenge and revealed their location, he would gently slip the net underneath them, and, when in place, swiftly lift it up and add another frog to his tin. They would fetch a couple of shillings each at the high school, but mostly they were added to the frog pond at home and remained there to swell the nightly chorus.

Other days consisted of catching freshwater lobsters, then cooking them in a tin can on a small fire. On these days he would lie on his back in the warm sun, watching the clouds scudding by against the vivid blue of a South Island sky, and wistfully muse in a Tom Sawyer/Huck Finn kind of way, that one could survive in the wild if it came down to it, escaping the painful world of adults altogether.

The Boy's foraging on these adventures also included seasonal mushrooms, turnips, potatoes, alfalfa stalks, crab-apples, plumbs, blackberries and apples, all available if one knew where and when to look, and the farmer wasn't too vigilant.

This was also the age when The Boy discovered carbide, a grey powdery-surfaced rock, which, when wetted, gave off highly flammable acetylene gas. This magical substance was legally able to be purchased by young boys from hardware stores in Dunedin. He had acquired a carbide lamp. A wondrous brass construction designed to be worn on a miner's helmet. It consisted of two chambers;

the upper chamber, a small water tank with its filling cap and adjustable regulator valve, allowing the water to be dripped at a measured rate into the lower chamber, which contained the small rocks of carbide. The combining of the two, the water and the carbide, gave off the acetylene gas. This gas fed back up a thin tube to a ceramic and brass nipple in the centre of a polished brass mirror. But to a young boy, a small flickering flame was nothing compared to an explosion.

First off, he obtained a sturdy Chelsea Golden Syrup tin with a press-on lid, then, with the aid of a small brad, pierced a hole in the bottom near the rim of the can. Precious pebbles of carbide were dropped in the tin and a generous gob of saliva was deposited on top. The lid was quickly pressed into place and the tin laid on its side with a foot holding it firm. When a small wisp of white gas appeared from the hole, a lit match was presented with glorious results. It became a matter of pride as to how loud the resulting explosion was and how far the lid was blown. But inevitably, in the reasoning of a young boy, if small was good then big could only be better.

It came to pass that one day, as The Boy was exploring the local sheep drafting pens and drenching race, he came across a discarded large square plastic sheep drench container.

Now this would make a very loud explosion, he thought, as he checked his cache of carbide stones. Taking the container, he dipped its opening in the creek and scooped in a generous gulp of water, next followed a small handful of pea-sized carbide pebbles. *This ought to be good*, he decided.

His growing excitement alternated with fear as he screwed on the plastic cap leaving just a little play for the acetylene gas to displace the air. He set the container on the bank of the stream and waited for the telltale wisp of white gas to appear. An hour long minute passed with no visible result, so The Boy approached the container and removed the cap. Peering in, he could see the white gas swirling halfway up the container. He reasoned that the carbide was spent, so, standing a measured distance back, he struck a match and pitched it at the open mouth of the container. It missed, so a half step closer and another match, this one hit the rim. He repeated the process, inching closer each time. A match, fully lit, disappeared into the container. He tried once more with the same result.

This isn't going to work, he thought, being vaguely aware of 'combustion critical' gas to air ratios. So, standing squarely over the opening, he dropped a lit match down the throat of the plastic drum. The result was immediate and not at all pleasant. It was as if all the Tom Thumbs, Jumping Jacks, Double

Happys, Sky Rockets, Roman Candles and Bunsen Burners he had ever abused, were roaring their flaming, jet-engine-exhaust-vengeance full in his face. He staggered into the creek, fell to his knees and plunged his face into the water. He lifted his head out to gasp a lungful of air and plunged it under again.

The next half hour was spent progressively lengthening the periods between submersions and increasingly fretting about how he was going to face his parents' wrath. The internal darkness answered with a frightening immediacy, and suicide once again presented itself as an option as his long history of shame and failings flooded his mind.

He need not have worried; his father didn't beat him for this incident. He considered the lobster red face, burnt ears and loss of hair, eyebrows and eye lashes sufficient punishment, and sent his son off to school the next day as usual, to explain his appearance as best he could.

Another source of explosive delight was to be had from a length of one inch diameter cold rolled mild steel bar, known simply as a banger. This was a language clearly understood by twelve year old boys of a certain nature. It required that a hole be drilled in from one end, a whisker bigger than the diameter of and about half the length of a four inch nail. It only remained for, say, half a dozen of the heads from wooden safety matches to be scraped into the hole and cautiously tamped down. The flat cut nail was then carefully inserted and the whole device inverted and the nail head stuck smartly on a hard surface. The resultant very loud bang was both a joy in itself and a source of kudos from one's peers.

The Boy also delighted in making shanghais. One could be assembled in less than half an hour. It only required the leather tongue from a pair of shoes – not too hard to come by as the uppers always outlasted the rest of the shoe – a short length of string and a strip of rubber from an inner tube.

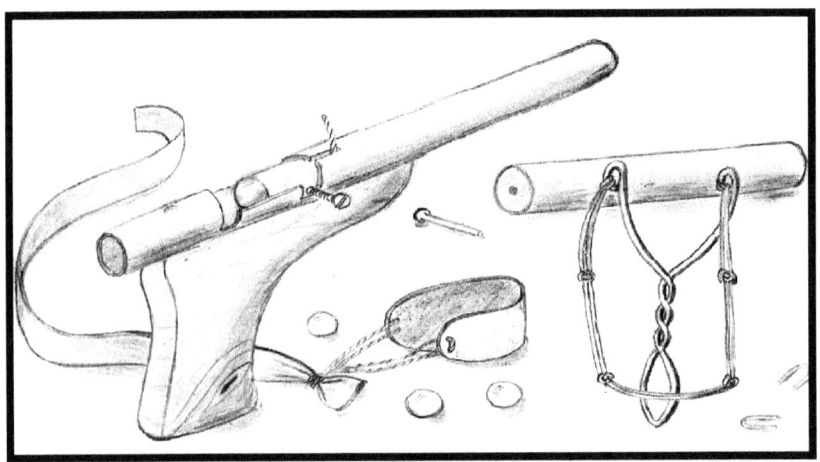

Left to right: shanghai, cracker gun, banger, staple shanghai.

A more vicious version was the staple shanghai, formed from the ubiquitous number eight wire and three or five rubber bands, the uneven number to provide a knot-free launch point. The Boy devised a simple jig to make his own staples, a cost saving move as money was never freely available and usually had to be accounted for, as did the strange U shaped welts appearing on he and his friends' bodies.

A more sophisticated device, which required more skill and care to build was a cracker gun. This was fashioned from a length of small bore piping; the trick being to find a steel bar which would fit snugly inside the pipe. Then, with little more than a good eye, a steady hand, a drill and a sharp hacksaw, a fully functioning pistol could be constructed. The pipe was notched out to accept the 'bolt' formed by the bar, a slit cut in the top of the piping barrel to allow the wick of the cracker to be lit. The stock was usually formed from the end piece of a fruit box since these were always readily available and easy to work.

Then came sourcing a suitable supply of projectiles, best of course were steel ball bearings. If obtainable, they were usually reserved for an enclosed area such as a garage or basement where they could be retrieved for reusing. Failing that, anything which fitted down the barrel would do, the more snug the fit, the better the result. These guns endowed the owner with an aura of respect and fear and were greatly valued. Needless to say, The Boy considered he had the best one among his peers.

6 Turning Points

The Boy was surprised to find himself somewhere he never expected to be; high school. It wasn't so much that he didn't intend to arrive there. He had presumed something would have intervened. He simply hadn't imagined himself living that long.

He saw his life as resembling an endless game of rugby. He had been made to play the sport as a very young boy and had always found it confusing and full of incomprehensible rules. He stumbled along in the rear, hoping no one would pass him the ball as he didn't have a clue what to do with it; that was also how he experienced life.

Nowadays, he would probably have been diagnosed with ADHD and medicated. He had a chaotic internal world and an inability to maintain any semblance of calm focus or concentration. As a result, he was a disruptive influence in class, and that, combined with a slightly cowered air, fear of authority, and parents who never contacted the school or attended PTA meetings, made him a perfect target for those teachers with a sadistic bent, or perhaps those who had just had a bad day. He quickly broke the record for canings. One particularly vicious P.E. teacher always caned him in his thin cotton gym shorts. Once he had to secretly soak his underpants off his buttocks when they were welded with blood to this split skin.

In all his school years, he had never mastered the art of quiet compliance, and with a mind that darted off in a hundred different directions at once, he found himself for days on end, just as at primary school, with his desk in the corridor outside the principal's office.

Also, as at primary school, his attempts at forming more than superficial relationships with the opposite sex never got off the ground. He didn't like himself, so how could anyone else? Any attempt from others at a compliment or closeness, he saw as a threat and treated it with distain growing from the soil of distrust. To drop his guard was fraught with fears of vulnerability and emotional pain; better to remain apart.

High school was punctuated with regular incidents of questionable judgement, as well as being the class clown. He would occasionally excel himself such as when he brought a large bottle of

French Dry Gin to school. He had found it stashed in the cellar; his father often did this in an attempt to smuggle alcohol past his mother. He took it, safe in the knowledge that his father would either think he had already drunk it or have forgotten he had put it there in the first place. It was sufficient to get he and a couple of others in his class very noticeably affected. The teachers suspected illness and notified the parents. Later, when the truth came out, he received the inevitable hiding, this one intensified by both his mother's annoyed embarrassment and his father's guilt at being the unwitting supplier. The Boy figured it had been worth it for the esteem he gained in some of his peers' eyes.

An even less wise action saw him place and set a gin trap in his school locker. That earned him both a caning and a hiding, but he never got his lunch stolen again.

The years stuttered by, he was sixteen, and had not achieved at high school. He had sat the school certificate exam over each of two successive yearly attempts. The first time, when to obtain the certificate, one had to accrue a total number of points over several subjects. The second attempt was after a criteria change, and one could pass, subject by subject. So, in his mind, by combining the two years, he had succeeded, but not in the opinion of those who granted such things.

An uncertain future loomed.

One evening as he was preparing to walk down to the local shops to buy a Mother's Day present, he glanced into the lounge to see his father contorted on the couch with face grey and lips blue. He ran in to a strange choking gurgle, hooked a piece of apple from his father's throat, pulled him onto the floor and began administering CPR. He shouted to his mother to call an ambulance. She stood in the kitchen doorway, telling him to get a towel because "I don't want him throwing up on the carpet". He repeated his request and she hers. Realising she was in shock, he phoned for an ambulance himself and returned to resuscitating his father until the ambulance crew arrived to take over, but the extended history of heart attacks had taken its toll. They were too late. He died in his son's arms.

The Boy

Why did you call me 'The Boy', Dad?
Why didn't you use my name?
By calling me 'The Boy', Dad,
did it make me more easy to blame?

Did it lessen the weight of your fists, Dad?
Did it distance the man from the deed?
Or ease the sting of knowing, Dad,
that I was not your seed?

Is that why you never talked to me?
What did you think that would do?
Would it melt the ice in your eyes, Dad,
to know that I loved you?

You crushed the heart of a child, Dad,
you stifled the soul of a youth.
A lie gets heavy with time, Dad,
better to face the truth.

If… you were not my father,
and I was not your son,
you could still have loved me,
we would both have won.

You could have protected me,
and safe within your arms,
have fended off the predators,
and all their evil charms.

His father's death brought an end to the constant wounding, of Idiot! Fool! Nincompoop! ringing in his ears, but he could have put up with that a little longer, because sixteen was too young to lose your dad. That loss was compounded by his mother's accusation that he had killed his father, that it was his worrying behaviour that had brought about his father's death. That often repeated accusation placed a burden of guilt on his shoulders that he never fully shrugged off.

Three days after his father's death, The Boy experienced a very powerful spiritual force. It had the presence and feel of a heavy velvet blanket of impenetrable blackness. He never saw it with his physical eyes, but he had no doubt of its reality. It lowered from above and settled over him. It was palpable, gentle but unstoppable, he felt it descend upon his life and upon his spirit.

This was not the first time that he had felt another realm intruding into his. He remembered an occasion when the family had been holidaying in an area they had never been before, and were driving around looking for the camping ground. He told them when and where to turn, and added that there was a tennis court just around the corner. He didn't know how he knew, but sure enough there it all was. The family distanced him even more after that.

The Boy continued to experience an unrelenting pull and drawing toward acts and situations of personal danger. On one occasion he and a group of friends found themselves in Roxburgh, a town in Central Otago, noted among other things for its hydro electric dam. It was at this dam that The Boy once again flirted with eternity. The dam was a gravity type, in that at an appropriate place on the Clutha River, its massive flow was stopped and allowed to build up behind an immense concrete wall, the water being then released down to eight huge metal pipes, or penstocks, and its falling force harnessed to spin turbines and generate electricity for the New Zealand power grid.

To the side of the penstocks were three spillways, which allowed excess water to be released down the face of the dam and off on its restless way. These spillways, angled at about forty five degrees, were opened when there was too much water behind the dam, and either the penstocks generating-ability was not required or they were already running to full capacity. On the day of their visit, the Clutha was running high following days of rain, the dam was over full and the massive steel shutter at the top of one of the spillways was winched high to allow the tons of water to proceed on its unstoppable journey to the Pacific Ocean.

As the huge volume of water erupted through the gated opening in the top of the dam, it arched out into space before crashing back into its concrete chute. This spectacular display of raw power and potential danger drew The Boy like a magnet. The others all stayed a sensible distance back from the safety rail flanking the concrete roadway, which ran along the top of the dam as it spanned the mighty Clutha River.

Looking out over the safety rail down into the roiling tumult was, of course, not sufficient for The Boy, so he mounted the rail, and, not being satisfied with balancing on the barrier dripping wet with spray thrown up by the cascade, The boy lowered himself down and hung from the bottom of the fence. The squeals from the girls in the party only served to inspire him and so he gripped with one hand and waved at his horrified audience with the other. He hung for a few seconds, one slip away from what would be a long fall into a speeding torrent of water, which rapidly became, at the foot of the spillway, a churning pool from which there would be no surviving.

Following his father's death, the local G.P. had prescribed tranquilisers to his mother and him. He didn't ask for them, he didn't think he needed them, but there they were, so he dutifully took them. They were to mark a turning point in his life. The drugs worked their magic. Suddenly he felt OK, suddenly he felt there could be a point and a purpose to life. His horizon lifted, brightened, and stretched outthis experience to stop, but it did. The course of medication ceased, but he had tasted a different reality, colour had briefly come back into his world. further than he could have imagined. He could not remember ever feeling this way.

Roxburgh Hydro Electric Dam (The yellow dump truck sits on the roadway above the three spillways) photographs courtesy of Wikipedea.

Below: The Spillways: (note the steel shutters and the stains showing a common volume of water).

He did not want this experience to stop, but it did. The course of medication ceased, but he had tasted a different reality, colour had briefly come back into his world.

He began to seek out drugs.

It didn't take him long to find them. His first marijuana experience was a mixed one. Having smoked cigarettes from the age of ten he was well used to drawing smoke down to his lungs. However, this was a different technique. Instead of first using one's mouth as a reservoir, then drawing the smoke and air mixture down, with marijuana it was drawn down directly in order to minimise the dilution and maximise the effect.

At first he felt nothing, then a slight tingling over his stomach that had an almost sexual element, this element rapidly spreading throughout his body, accompanied by a swiftly growing sense of unreality and an irrepressible urge to giggle. Colours took on a vibrancy, and sounds, a clarity never before experienced. His ability to gauge the passage of time was lost, with a minute stretching out to an uncertain length.

These were the pleasant effects. What tarnished the pleasure was his loss of ability to judge the mood, read the body language and know the intent of others. This was an area of extreme importance to The Boy, and to lose that was to dwell in very frightening and unsafe territory. But it was not enough to stop or even slow his exploration into the world of drugs.

He left school, joined the work force, finding a job as a warehouseman. He was good at it and enjoyed the work. He was promoted to travelling salesman, but his damaged state and recreational drug use served to sabotage his performance. A foolish accident in which he wrote off the company car and at the same time cut off the telephone lines between Roxburgh and Alexandra, combined with falling sales figures, had his employer suggesting he might be better suited to a different career.

He applied for a job as one of a three man contract fencing team. He hoped, to a degree, that since this job was in the country and miles from anywhere, it might provide the opportunity to free himself from the drug scene. But it felt as if the die was cast; he could not shake off the darkness and despair within; his mental health was on the decline.

The cumulative weight of woundings, which had begun virtually at birth, were becoming harder and harder for him to cope with. The drug use was a symptom as much as a cause, it was an escape from the pain of being him, and from a life which was becoming progressively more unbearable. The escape they provided, however, was repaid with interest, as the emotional instability, enmeshment and dependency steadily increased. Inevitably, he lost his job as a contract fencer through being unable to match the other two's performance in what was a very physically demanding occupation, although he was the only person the gang boss had ever known to be able to lift a concrete strainer post, unaided, out of a too shallow posthole.

Around this time he did a brief stint as a construction labourer, and the inner presence he had grown used to began to show itself in the form of abilities he knew were not his. As the new boy on site, it was his duty to make the tea, take lunch orders and fetch them from local shops.

One day as he was swilling out the large teapot prior to lunch, one of the workmen approached him and ordered his food, proffering money as he did so. The Boy mildly protested that he did not have his notepad with him as more workmen wandered over, all stating their requirements. He took orders from six workers, each placing orders for pies and sandwiches, and also for cakes and buns, the latter of which had to be purchased from a separate store.

He put the water on to boil and walked to the two stores, purchasing from the first shop, six different savoury orders from six different amounts of money, all held together in the same pocket. Then walked to the next store, buying six separate lots of sweet items, paying from the remainder of each workers' change.

He then walked back to the 'smoko' shed, handing out everyone's correct order, along with their correct change. No one seemed to notice, but The Boy was well aware that he had just performed a feat quite beyond him.

This 'photographic' memory appeared again at a party he attended. He led the 'crew' into a student flat party they had been invited to, and entered the lounge ahead of his friends. They had been smoking dope before they drove there so he was well and truly stoned. The student friend and host did a round of names as The Boy stood in the middle of the circle of seated faces. When The Boy's friends filed into the room, he rattled off the fifteen full names in perfect order.

"Oh, no," said one of the students, "he's one of them!" which received a chuckle from the stunned observers.

He gained employment at the local freezing works, working one season in the casings department. It was dirty, smelly work but with the whole department on contract, they worked hard, finished the day early and were very well paid. However, the contract team did not want him back for another season. His behaviour had become increasingly bizarre, he was losing his ability to contain himself to what was normal, pleasant and socially appropriate. His next season was spent in what was known as the slipe room. This was a department one floor below the killing chain. The flesh piece from the face and ears of the sheep was sluiced down a chute from the floor above and went through a ten yard long, four foot diameter, steel cylinder. This cylinder was supported on rollers and was on a slight slope. It had an internal sprinkler pipe and rows of fixed steel fins, a little like the bowl of a concrete mixer.

The whole giant device rotated, and its purpose was to thoroughly wash, rinse and deliver into a wooden barrow, the face pieces or slipes from the sheep. These were then gathered by two workers, cut in half on a mounted blade, and loaded into a hopper, which cooked them and removed the small amount of wool they held. All in all, the job was mind-numbing.

This, of course, lent itself to more drug use. The Boy's co-worker was a burned out hippy, complete with the obligatory pony tail, so was a perfect mentor and guide into the deeper world of drugs. This was the era of Timothy Leary and his *Electric Cool Aid Acid Test* notoriety, and his avocation to America and the world, to *Turn on, tune in and drop out*, so, in short order, he was introduced to LSD.

It was a Saturday afternoon in Dunedin. The Boy had ridden into town on his motorbike and was ready for his first 'trip' as the LSD experience was called. Marijuana is about seven times stronger in the present day than it once was, but conversely, LSD was about six times stronger then than it is now. This particular trip was in the form of a tiny square of gelatine impregnated with the substance. It was called 'clear light' and dissolved quickly on the tongue.

The two drank coffee and talked as they waited for the drug to take effect. Right on cue, around the twenty minute mark, it began with a very pleasant tingling over his stomach, the now familiar marijuana-like sexual thrill, this spreading quickly to send mild waves flushing through his entire body. Then the similar marijuana feeling of unreality began.

But the sense of clarity experienced on marijuana was as nothing compared to this! Sounds, colours, touch, smell, all were electric in their intensity. They became exaggerated to the point where he became lost in the sheer yellowness of a buttercup; it filled his eye, his mind, and taxed his ability to contain its beauty within his comprehension. Its magnificence simply overwhelmed him.

Then there was music. His co-worker from the freezing works owned a very good sound system and reverently placed on the turntable a vinyl recording of the Rolling Stones. He carefully lined up a track called *'Angie'* and turned up the volume. From the first hiss and crackle of the stylus on the vinyl, it entranced him, the poignant opening guitar chords made him gasp, the wistful strings brought tears to his eyes, Mick Jagger's aching lyrics of love lost tore holes in his heart. All held him captive and sent him swooping and soaring through the emotional journey of the song, finally casting him abruptly back down to earth as the last notes faded.

He fell in love with the experience ... and the drug.

The whole trip lasted some ten hours or so. He rode home and finally drifted off in his own bed to the bizarre experience of an endless succession of distorted faces streaming toward him whenever he closed his eyes. But close his eyes he did, and eventually drifted off to sleep. He woke the next morning with the knowledge that something profound had changed in his mind, a switch had been flipped, a switch that could never be unflipped.

He had listened to several music groups that night, but one in particular was to capture his imagination, and in the months and years to follow, have the most influence on his life, a group called Pink Floyd. They captured the emotions he felt, but could never have expressed in music. Specifically, an album entitled *'Dark Side of the Moon'*, which was to accompany him on his journey into insanity.

7   Flights of Fancy

Saturday mornings at the freezing works were often given to catching up on any loose ends from the previous day. His department, trailing behind the killing chain on the floor above, did a thorough clean up, part of this clean up involving the huge steel washing cylinder. What had also become almost routine was for The Boy and his co-worker to 'drop half a trip' of LSD to add interest to the chore.

This week it was his co-workers turn to clean the cylinder. The protocol, carefully designed to avoid accidents, involved hanging a printed *'Do not use'* warning sign on the two switches, which operated the spinning steel tube. These switches were two feet apart and had to be pushed simultaneously to start the cylinder tumbling. Alongside them was another push button that started the powerful and noisy pump, which forced water at high pressure through the internal sprinklers mounted inside the length of the pipe. Cleaning this machine required that a worker crawl inside the tube and manually remove any slipes snagged on the internal blades and sprinklers.

The Boy waited until his friend was at the farthest depth into the tube, knowing he was 'tripping' and that therefore his judgment was compromised and his emotions intensified, knowing also that his friend would have difficulty hearing, both from being inside the tube and also because of the general noise of the department.

He called down the tube, "You alright mate, everything OK?"

"Yes, fine thanks," came the echoing reply.

"What?" The Boy said. "You want me to turn it on?"

"No!" came back the frightened response.

"OK then, I'll turn it on," shouted back The Boy.

"No! No!" his terrified friend yelled from the depths of the machinery.

"OK, here we go!" shouted back The Boy, as he pushed the switch which operated the sprinklers.

The noisy water pump thumped into life, accompanied by a shriek of horror as his co-worker imagined his grisly and imminent death. The Boy turned off the pump and convulsed with laughter as his traumatised co-worker, scrambling backwards, shot out from the washer. They took an extended smoko break. It was during one of these breaks that they introduced what was probably the oldest worker in the freezing works to marijuana. He was a gentle soul who meandered about picking up, tidying, sweeping, and just generally doing all those things that made sure the department ticked over smoothly. He enjoyed the effects of the smoke and sometimes joined the two for a quiet joint.

On one of these occasions, he shared an experience he had been carrying for a very long time. He had been doing his tidying and was a little late for his meal break, but decided to empty his barrow before joining the others in the lunch room, so he wheeled it as always toward the chute room where all organic waste eventually ended up.

This waste consisted of the cooked slipes, the occasional organ which had mistakenly slipped down the many processing line chutes from the killing chain above, and also included the odd sheep head which had thudded and banged its way along the length of the slipe washing tube. Nothing was wasted; it was cooked, rendered down, ground up, dried and bagged into fertiliser.

As the cleaner rounded the corner, he saw a small circle of men grouped around the floor chute, and through the gaps between them, saw a pair of legs, still in their boots, disappear down the hole.

Realising that no one had seen him or heard his rubber wheeled trolley and gumboots over the ambient noise, he quickly backed out and never spoke of the incident,'til then. As far as the police investigation knew, the missing man had left work at lunchtime and was never seen again.

Another escapade occurred one winter's day when The Boy found himself stranded at a friend's house overnight due to snow. Next morning, the phone rang. It was his workmate asking if he was free for the day. He was and was picked up in his friend's car. As they drove off he asked what was happening. The response was an extended hand, which dropped a selection of pills into his.

"Take these. We're on our way to Taieri Airport. The guys have hired a seven seater Piper Cherokee and we're going to Fiordland for lunch."

The Boy swallowed the pills and sat back in the sports car as his mentor turned up the stereo in the two seater V12 Daimler Dart convertible, and started on the drive to the airport. Half an hour into the drive, the pills were taking effect. Among them was obviously some LSD as he felt the now familiar symptoms of the hallucinogen, one of which was the phenomena whereby what one 'thought' became what one 'saw', that is, the internal reality becomes the external reality.

One track on the stereo was the brand new Led

Zeppelin's *'Stairway to Heaven'*. Under the influence of the acid, The Boy envisioned a stairway extending in front of them, and in a perfectly serious but rather worried and amazed voice, asked the driver if he really felt the car could negotiate what was clearly a very steep set of stairs directly in front of them.

They arrived at the airport to a rather odd gathering of people, introductions were made, hireage fees were paid, and they all clambered aboard. The Piper Cherokee taxied into position and the group was cautioned not to talk, especially about drugs, while the pilot spoke with the control tower and accelerated to take off speed. The Boy had managed to secure the prime seat next to the pilot and began asking about the plane's capabilities and whether the pilot had experienced negative 'G' forces. This comment was to feature later in the flight.

The flight was amazing, the pilot was the only person not 'tripping', but he was certainly stoned, as joint after joint was passed around the cabin. Someone had brought a portable stereo; it was turned up loud to reach over the sound of the engines and the wind noise. All in all it made a heady mix combined with the drugs, one of which he was later told was psilocybin, the hallucinogenic mushroom. Another was Valium and another Benzedrine. Also by this stage, alcohol was being passed around. As they approached the Southern Alps, the pilot decided to see how close he could get to them without actually touching the snow covered slopes. A couple of vagrant wind gusts shunted them perilously near and discouraged further attempts.

Safely over the pass, the pilot recalled the mention of negative G's and began a manoeuvre, which he had to later mime with props over lunch at the Milford Hotel, as all ability to track the planes convolutions was shortly to desert The Boy.

It seemed the pilot brought the plane's nose up and climbed at full throttle until it hung vertically motionless in the sky, unable to make any more headway. It began dropping quite some distance, sliding tail first, then the pilot sent it over backwards and down into a startlingly steep dive directly earthward. The Boy watched as his packet of cigarettes and box of matches lifted off his lap, drifted over his head, and floated lazily to the rear of the plane.

Then, too slowly, the nose of the screaming plane came up and levelled off above the shoreline, at such a low altitude that the surf spray required the use of the windscreen wiper.

"How's that for negative G's?" asked the pilot.

No answer was forthcoming.

8 A Little Paranoia

The Boy had always been somewhat prone to a certain instability, but given his circumstances this was not surprising. He could remember back to times when, as a child, he would be gripped by an anxious conviction that, unless he got out of bed and quickly ran three times around the house, something un-named but terrible would befall both he and his family. He had a number of these compulsions, but managed to indulge them without being observed.

Most of them revolved around ritualistically counting, or repeating actions a magical number of times. One particularly bizarre one took him by surprise and, sadly, had it been spotted, may have brought him the medical attention he needed.

He was heading to the local shop when he felt compelled to walk in a straight line, not too odd in itself, however this straight line necessitated him walking over several cars. This he did, springing nimbly up the boots, over the roofs and along the bonnets. Thankfully, at the time, he was a lot lighter and cars were a lot stronger. If he was observed, it was never mentioned.

He also worried deeply about things which should not trouble a young boy, things such as whether his parents were really his parents, and the startling resemblance atomic structures bore to solar systems, that perhaps our entire universe was just a meaningless speck of dust in God's eye, and therefore held just as much importance. Songs also worried him, after all there were a limited number of notes and only a certain number of words; they must run out sometime. Another thought which had worried him for some time was that if God was eternal, then perhaps, over time, He had become senile and the whole of creation was out of His control. It often seemed that way.

With his father now dead and his two elder brothers having moved out of home, he was left with his lonely and unstable mother. His home situation became more and more untenable, under she of the mixed messages, the master of the double bind, the dispenser of guilt, an example of which might be her habit of asking, in a thinly disguised injured tone, if he was going out that night, when plainly he had showered and dressed to do so. If he asked would she prefer he stay at home, she would protest that he should go out and enjoy himself, that she would be fine, left at home, on her own. Either way, if he stayed home or if he went out, he was in the wrong.

A further area of pressure and one which he had a difficult time coming to terms with, was the way she had begun insisting he garden and mow the lawns without his shirt on, and made much of bringing him drinks and watching him work, especially when a particular female friend of hers was visiting. He only accepted his disturbing suspicions when they were also raised by a friend.

Several of his friends, fellow drug users, had rented a large flat in Dunedin's High Street. The flat had seen better days and better tenants. It had four bedrooms, two lounges, a separate kitchen and dining room and several fireplaces, all fitted with bell pushes alongside to summon the servants. There was an additional bedroom out the back to house staff.

The friends agreed, with some trepidation, to The Boy joining them, as his reputation for drug taking and alcohol consumption as well as a somewhat eccentric personality was a concern. His consumptions steadily increased, as did his eccentricity.

The parties were something to behold. The many

and various talents of the flatmates were drawn on, and the flat became decked out with a number of bizarre oddities as befits a group indulging in the exploration of LSD. The corridor was illuminated from one end with a spotlight set behind a revolving disc of coloured lenses, powered with a liberated oven rotisserie motor. A large pair of polished stainless steel mirrors was set on opposite sides of the wide hallway and deliberately distorted to have a disorienting effect on passersby.

LSD fuelled hallucinations were based on an extended and exaggerated version of whatever was in one's mind at the time, so any altered external reality added to this effect. A very good sound system was set up with speakers in both lounge rooms. The drugs flowed freely and it had become a matter of pride for The Boy to have a selection on hand. All in all, it had become a party house, and was to provide the setting for his deterioration into madness.

It was difficult to say when The Boy's distrust of adults drifted into general paranoia. As a child, he had a very strong sense of justice and honesty and, as a young and disillusioned boy, had long ago made a conscious decision not to trust grownups; an early disillusionment he recalled was when he discovered the truth about that cruel Santa Clause myth sold to children in the name of some sort of misplaced parental indulgence. He could still remember the feeling of betrayal with the realisation that his parents and most other adults had lied to him for all those years; he found it unforgivable.

Sleigh Me

Don't tell me there's a Santa,
just tell it to me straight.
Just say it's generosity,
we yearly celebrate.

That once a long long time ago,
in a far and distant land,
a kindly man distributed
some gifts he'd made by hand.

It gladdened all the children's hearts,
and filled his own with joy,
knowing he'd brought happiness,
to every girl and boy.

So keep your flying reindeer,
on their supersonic flights,
your fairies, elves and pixies,
in their bright green satin tights.

It's kindness we commemorate,
it's openness of heart,

*it's giving gifts, it's joy and love,
and that's just for a start.*

*So, don't tell me there's a Santa,
then grind my heart to dust,
don't tell me there's a Santa,
and then, expect my trust!*

The events in his early life only served to reinforce this distrust. A little paranoia could be quite useful such as when he brought out his stash of marijuana and its paraphernalia, papers, lighter, roach clip, etc. All kept in a large coffee jar. He would slide the jar swiftly down the table directly at any new member of the growing circle of smokers who then had no choice but to catch it, with the instruction to 'check it out!' Then he would receive it back being careful to hold it only by the serrations on the plastic lid and by the bands of dimpled glass.

Large joints were rolled and smoked. At this point, when the 'new boy' was well and truly stoned and the jar had been returned to its cache, he would be advised that discretion would be wise as his finger prints were now all over the jar and The Boy's were not.

But whenever it happened, the transition from a healthy caution around people's intentions into doubting everyone and everything, it was now building, fuelled by the dope smoking, and was beginning to get in the way of normal social functioning. He began to second guess all. As others started picking up on his overly suspicious attitude and sought to reassure him it only compounded the situation, he read their reassurances as paternalistic and false, designed to throw him off the track. It became self fulfilling as his paranoia caused others to talk about him, and their discussions aside about his increasingly odd behaviour were, to him, proof of conspiracy.

He was now also experiencing what he was later to learn were 'ideas of reference'. Newspapers, radio, television, all began to be rife with special messages meant for him. He became very stressed and applied more and more emotional energy into trying to unravel the cosmic mystery that he was being led, by these cryptic hints, into uncovering.

His regular drug taking now included LSD. One Saturday night, which had become a regular time for 'dropping a trip', he was again pushing the boundaries of his risk-taking behaviours by taking more than others. He would now, as a matter of course, take two maybe four trips. Another aspect of those early 'acid days' was that since LSD was an extremely concentrated substance, it was very difficult to produce regular measured doses. Also, the source of supply would vary. Consequently, the strength and precise composition of the 'trip' was never the same from one shipment to the next.

This particular Saturday night he had taken a strong batch. The trip started out in the usual way with the gentle waves of pseudo-sexual pleasure rippling outward from his solar plexus, followed by the sudden sharpening of all his senses. The colours from the spotlight in the hall washing through the house, making the walls look almost edible, the ethereal sounds of Pink Floyd swirling from the multiple speakers, all adding to the unreality of his building hallucinogenic experience. As the 'trip' progressed, he went to the hallway and hid off to the side in a large broom cupboard in the bathroom. With the door open the merest crack he could see people passing in the hall. This became a hugely amusing game. As they passed he would call their name in a loud whisper, and convulse in fits of suppressed laughter as they turned to find no one, and watch as they stood in confused puzzlement before walking on.

One party goer, after a couple of these experiences, started toward his hiding place. In an instant The Boy pulled the door closed and waited for the victim of his game to move on. However, with the door closed and total darkness ensuing, the LSD hallucinations, exploded into a bamboozling display of total confusion, as whatever he thought immediately became what he saw, and with no actual visual stimulation his mind was open to generate what it wished. He stood in a swirling cloud of bewildering images. Although he was standing in a storage closet less than an arm span in either direction, he was unable to hold his mind together long enough to retain the memory as to which wall he had just pushed on to establish whether it was the door or not, and which wall he was yet to try. After what seemed like a very long time, a 'wall' moved, became the door and he stepped out and back into the party. This was going to be a long night.

The LSD he had taken was proving to be the strongest he had ever used. So of course, he decided to amplify the experience with dope. He sat in a large lounge chair, drew down generously on an offered joint and waited for the THC elevator to kick in and take him up another few thousand feet. He did not have to wait long. He found his surroundings retreating, no that was not the right term. They didn't become physically distant, they became less distinct, less real, his ability to understand them diminished, they were still there but his capacity to identify, recognise and make sense of them ceased. His mind was shrinking inward upon itself, completely losing the facility to process external information, even sound; his ears could hear it but his mind could not receive it. This continued. His field of awareness became smaller and smaller until he became merely a point of consciousness. In fact it was quite a struggle to hold even that thought.

He sat there in his chair not knowing anything, not perceiving anything, having no thoughts whatsoever. When later he was to come across the Zen concept of 'no mind' he would easily identify with that state. As he sat, he began to be aware of his existence, but it was perhaps what a newborn might understand in that he looked down at his arms and legs but didn't yet think of them as 'his'. He had no context to place them in and was unable to distinguish where he finished and where the world began. He looked around the room and saw that there were moving objects and that they bore a resemblance to him. He discovered that he was able to move his arm and established that he and the chair were separate. This was a revelation, albeit a brief one as once more his mind withdrew into itself and he was again merely a point of consciousness, hovering, lost in time and space. This process repeated itself with progressively longer periods of self awareness and greater levels of understanding.

At one stage when someone leaned over and spoke to him, he was unable to reply as he had only just managed to solidify the knowledge that the other moving objects in the room were separate sentient beings like him, human. It would be some time before he retrieved the memory that they each could expel air through their mouths and form puffs of breath, which were able to be picked up via ears as sounds, decoded by the other and so communicate meaning.

All this as he visually hallucinated and people and things morphed into many and various forms. If, for instance, someone struck him as looking a little horse-like, then that would be the appearance they assumed, complete with tossing mane and flaring nostrils, until his mind moved on.

He also experienced what he would later term retinal retention, the optical effect where images would remain for a second or two, imprinted on the retina of his eye and, as objects moved or he shifted his gaze, his visual world would stretch and warp in an elastic cartoon-like manner.

A normal person would probably find this terrifying and an experience to be avoided. But with his background, his permanent level of distortion in his self-appraisal and social relationships, a 'trip' was a holiday. Time spent drugged was freedom from his steady state of mental and emotional pain.

This was all taking its toll and he steadily sank ever deeper into the mental quagmire. These drug induced experiences were passing, a few hours here a few hours there, the effects would wear off and he would resume normal life, well normal as he knew it, but the darkness inside was drawing him down, down toward a place he had never been before, a place of total madness.

9 The Forces Gather

The lunatic is in my head,
the lunatic is in my head.
You raise the blade, you make the change,
you re-arrange me 'til I'm sane.
You lock the door
and throw away the key,
There's someone in my head but it's not me.
© Pink Floyd 'Brain Damage' 1973

"I think I'm suffering from paranoid schizophrenia," he told the doctor.

"Really? What makes you think that?"

The Boy went on to give a rather detailed description of the condition and the corresponding symptoms he was experiencing but neglected to mention the drug taking.

"I'll arrange for you to see a psychiatrist," said the doctor.

This duly occurred and The Boy was introduced to the world of the theorists. This one practised what he would later come to know as Reflective Listening where he repeated back what the patient had told him with the intention of establishing understanding, clarity and rapport, but The Boy did not understand himself, or possess any clarity, so for him it was like talking to a tape recorder on delayed playback. That was not what he needed right now.

What he needed right now was answers. Answers to the endless stream of questions that flooded his mind. Answers as to why he felt the way he felt, thought the way he thought. Answers like how to respond to what he knew were spiritual forces growing and massing just through the veil, the veil which was becoming thinner and more transparent, less of a barrier between he and them, less of a divide between sanity and madness. They were gaining strength as he was losing it.

This doctor would have no idea what he was talking about. In that world he would be more lost than The Boy. The doctor's world was of biochemical imbalances, conditioned responses, and psycho-sexual complexes, that didn't allow for spiritual entities so The Boy didn't bother trying to explain. He was prescribed a couple of low dosage medications, which had the effect of smoothing out the troughs and crests of his increasingly fluctuating moods. This was merely treating the symptoms, but it was better than nothing.

Earlier, his quest to understand what was wrong with him, what was wrong with the world, his quest to make sense of anything, had led him to consume a bizarre range of books. He could not remember a time when he did not believe in some sort of Supreme Being, a Creator; it was the only thing which made any sense. The only thing which could explain the wondrous universe, from the spinning of a spider's web to the spinning of the planets. Whatever belief one started from, he reasoned, if worked backwards that belief must put forward an explanation for our existence. What naturally exists now, must have had a point of origin. Something cannot come from nothing. Therefore the origin of that something had to be outside of the natural, it had to be supernatural.

He saw Christianity as the logical extension of Judaism and the only belief system with both external and internal logic. But try as he might he could not 'get' The Bible, he could read the words, but they came to him as a collection of dry and dusty rules and regulations. One thing he had found that was clear, however, was God's opinion of sex between males. He had demonstrated that opinion in the destruction of the Old Testament towns of Sodom and Gomorrah. The Boy read that story several times; it only served to drive him deeper into himself, into his world of self loathing and his desire to be free.

As he reflected on his seduction, he came to the conclusion that he could never tell, because despite the prevailing wisdom, sexual abuse was worse for a boy than for a girl. A girl could tell. What was common to both was the obvious sense of violation due to any element of coercion or force employed, and of course, the betrayal of trust through an imbalance of ages or abuse of authority.

But that aside, his reasoning went something like this –

In sexual encounters it is usual for sexual acts to involve the opposite sex, not the same sex. It is also the cultural norm for the male to be the active/hunter and the female to be the passive/hunted, not the male to be the hunted. And critically, for a boy to be penetrated, is clearly not what biology intended, and for him this did more than make him doubt his maleness, it shattered his very sense of being. A girl victim received sympathy and comfort, her sexuality was never called into question. But it was the socially held notion that a boy must have somehow encouraged his sexual violation, that he was probably queer. Otherwise, how could he possibly let someone do that to him? It did not just cause him to wonder who he was, it caused him to wonder what he was. So, of course, he said nothing.

The rest of The Bible seemed devoid of anything inspiring and was about as interesting as the telephone directory. He became entranced by a series of novels by Lobsang Rampa, offering a path to spiritual enlightenment, until the author was exposed as a London plumber who had claimed a previous life as a Tibetan monk. Other sources of spiritual insight were offered by writers such as Carlos Castaneda and his encounters with the Yaqui Indian, Don Juan, who advocated Mexican hallucinogenic cacti. He had also taken to listening to religious groups addressing the passersby in Dunedin's 'Octagon' town centre.

The Boy's paranoid thoughts that he was being both talked about among people and secretly talked to in the media increased and began to steadily shift from a feeling to a belief. The psychiatrist he was seeing suggested he enter Waikari Hospital psychiatric ward for closer observation. He agreed to this and left arrangements to the hospital.

He had become convinced that there existed a worldwide conspiracy that he was not in on, and that it was his job, indeed his mission, to discover both what this was and his place within it. It also became clear in his thinking that there were enemies to this mission, enemies who must not discover what he did and did not know. His increasingly powerful delusional state began to express itself in odd ways, such as his belief that he could cure, with mind power, a case of tinea he had contracted. He also sat for protracted periods of time in front of the television set with it tuned to an unused channel and attempted to influence the random 'electronic snow' on the screen.

He often held council at the flat's kitchen table, expounding his increasingly bizarre theories to anyone who would listen, usually whilst high on marijuana or acid or both, and then later regretting his frankness. He started to believe that he was channelling 'evil vibes' from the spiritual dimension and attributed any negative happenings around him to this phenomenon, happenings such as faults in electrical equipment or events such as a friend's death in a motorcycle accident, even though he was nowhere near them.

His risk taking behaviours were getting worse. On one occasion he rode his Honda 250cc Motorsport at full throttle straight down High Street, one of the main arterial feeds into down town Dunedin. He rode squarely on the centre line and sped through the intersections without a chance of stopping. Traffic squealed to a halt and vehicles flashed their lights and sounded their horns. He laughingly roared by at 80 mph, and that only because the bike wouldn't go any faster. He had come to realise that he took such risks because the pain of living now outweighed his natural fear of death.

In an attempt to bring some sanity back into his life he decided to go on a one month drug fast. All went well with not so much as a Disprin passing his lips; the confusion subsided somewhat along with a degree of his anxiety. But there seemed to be quite a high base line of depression and paranoia which remained relatively unmoved.

On the last day of his month-long fast, the group went to the beach and were larking about. He found himself separated a little way from them when it happened. He sensed a spiritual presence approach, and then force itself into his mind. It was evil, it was malevolent, and it had just invaded the most personal space he had. It said nothing, it did nothing. But what was clear was that it was very powerful, and it was there to stay. His paranoia switched back on and all his anxiety along with it. As its mind met his mind he knew the stakes had just been raised, he was entering unknown territory, territory for which he had no map and no guide.

As he slipped deeper into mental illness, his strained and delusional mind began to divide and apportion power to words and groups of words. Positive power was associated with words such as good, up, white, right etc. and negative power was associated with their opposite: bad, down, black, left. He became very aware of, and mentally monitored, who used these words and in what context. These two forces, positive and negative were, he believed, in constant and deadly conflict. Indeed, the universe was engaged in a battle for supremacy. This he felt was the 'Great Truth' for which he had been searching.

But the weight of this knowledge and the absolutely vital importance of positioning himself in the correct place were too much for his bruised and battered psyche to bear. He felt that this battle for supremacy took place not only in the spiritual realm, but among human beings in the physical world as well, some of whom knew what was 'really going on'. But most, he thought, did not. How could he identify which were which, because since he knew this 'truth' others must also know. Who were they, how could he find out without 'blowing his cover'? His paranoia increased.

One day as he was being given a ride to the flat on the back of a friend's bike, they turned out of the freezing works yard straight into the path of an oncoming car, driven too fast, on the wrong side, by a drunken driver, directed he believed, to this place, at this time, by spiritual forces conspiring against him. His friend received a broken leg and bruising and an ambulance ride to hospital, he only a twisted ankle, but in his mind it was irrefutable and mounting evidence. They were clearly out to get him. But who could he turn to?

He phoned his mother but she was apparently not at home so he caught a taxi to Waikari Hospital Psychiatric ward and asked for the doctor he had been seeing. The doctor was not present so he confronted a female nurse and told her he had discovered the power of positive and negative thought and wished to discuss it with a psychiatrist. She left to summon one, glancing back apprehensively at this obviously raving nutter.

The psychiatrist arrived as The Boy stood surveying a painting by Hieronymus Bosch, renowned for his disturbing paintings. This one as usual depicted a dismembered but still alive human, overrun by tiny demons subjecting him to all sorts of intrusions and torments. Hardly the place for such a work, he thought. Unless of course the hospital was in on 'it' and were merely carrying out their part as agents of the negative forces.

The Boy talked to the psychiatrist, but amidst ramblings, told him he could not trust him and would seek the counsel of a priest as "Only a religious experience" could save him. The doctor suggested that they could summon one and that while waiting he could arrange a bed and something to relax him as he "appeared extremely agitated."

The Boy declined, suspecting ulterior motives.

With the speed of paranoid anxiety, he imagined a scenario in which the hospital was an agency that obtained unsuspecting and vulnerable people, drugged them, enabling them to drain their life force and substitute an entity from the 'other side', which would then go out into the world in the body of a previously trusted person to work evil.

He decided he would not wait for a priest if he was connected with that highly suspect hospital. He asked the hospital for a phone and contacted a religious group known as the Unification Church or 'Moonists' as they were also known, after their founder, Reverent Sun Myung Moon. He had talked to them in the town centre when they were having a rally in Dunedin's Octagon.

He took a taxi to their headquarters, noting that the taxi driver wore dark glasses on a dull day and wondering why.

He spoke to them a little about his beliefs, no longer theories, they agreed, and talked confidently of positive and negative forces. They also said they had been praying for "… another guy who didn't turn up" and whom they referred to as his "negative counterpart". They all entered the prayer room, he, as instructed, accident-injured leg first.

At last! Here were people who seemed to be on his wavelength, but he must be careful. No one, but no one, could be trusted! In the room was a photograph of Reverent Moon in profile. He noted that all the portraits in the house of the spiritual leader were of the reverend's same side. Was the spiritual leader hiding something?

10 Bishops and Bell Towers

The next day the group was due to travel to Wellington for a conference of the church. The Boy rang a friend, who drove them all to the railway station where a group of The Boy's friends saw them off. One of the Moonists, referring to the cars, made some quiet side comment about Satan prospering his followers, which brought more fear and confusion to The Boy. Were his friends really secret agents of Satan?

The trip north was uneventful for all except he, as his mind raced, over and over, trying to knit together the multiple threads of happenings into a meaningful shape. Sitting awake in the dark as the train clacked and rattled on it's journey, he prayed for a sign. This was seemingly answered with a 'falling star'. Was this an indication of his spiritual descent and if so, into what? He didn't know. Fear and confusion ratcheted up.

They arrived in Christchurch at the group house where they had a meal of left-over cakes begged from coffee shops. Were the cakes or the tea drugged? Again he didn't know, but his pupils were pinpricks in the bathroom mirror. The Boy showered and, following the strict instructions, went to bed in the room he had been shown, facing the way he had been shown. He drifted into a fitful sleep and awoke to the sound of their German Shepherd dog patrolling the pebbled path outside his window.

Then, surprisingly, one of the members of the group quietly opened the door, entered the room and slipped into the wardrobe. Odd behaviour, he thought, lying still and pretending not to notice. At that point, others began chanting in an adjoining room. His tired and tortured mind was unable to put this into any context so, in the dark, he began reciting The Lord's Prayer as well as he could remember and making the sign of the cross. After some time, someone else entered the bedroom, asking how he was. The man in the wardrobe slipped out under cover of this and both men retreated back into the body of the house, leaving The Boy to ponder the evening's events.

The next day, he told the girl whom he had initially contacted in Dunedin that he had decided to leave the sect and find his own path to truth. She pleaded for him to stay as "Theirs' was the only way". She cried, he cried, but left anyway, taking a taxi to the local Youth Hostel.

Being daytime, the Youth Hostel was not open and he had to wait. He considered baptising himself in the pool on the grounds, but his paranoid mind could not decide which 'side' had instituted fluoridation and what was the real reason behind it. He hung around and helped some workmen paint the hostel, mainly because they were using white paint.

Time passed and the hostel opened. He checked in with his last few dollars. He was allocated a bed which he swapped for a top bunk in line with his delusional state. He showered very thoroughly, performing every action three times, a number which had become fixed in his mind as a magical rite. He went through his suitcase and assembled a 'spiritual escape suit' consisting of exclusively white clothing: singlet, shirt, shorts and socks, all white. He wrapped these in a white towel and left to stash them.

His behaviours were becoming more bizarre by the hour as his mind came ever closer to its breaking point. If he had to make a turn to the left he came to a stop and, as if taking in the scenery, turned idly to his right on the spot, then, when he was facing the direction he needed to move in, he stepped forward on his way. He came upon the Avon River and stashed his 'spiritual suit' high in a tree, returning to the Youth Hostel by a circuitous route to shake off any followers.

At this point, The Boy was not eating. Even if he had had money he was too agitated to think of food. He went to bed and prayed, tossing and turning, but not in sleep. At about one a.m. he experienced what felt like a massive electrical shock slamming through his body, but without any pain.

Another resident asked, "What the hell was that?"

"I don't know," The Boy lamely replied, hopefully hiding his terror, but fully knowing it was another spiritual entity taking up residence in his body. He knew he had no defence against these occupations.

The Boy was stuck in Christchurch, his mind falling apart, his body, he believed, no longer solely his own, without money, without friends. He remembered his mother had said she was going to Amberly, a suburb of Christchurch, to stay with the boyfriend she had acquired after the death of her husband. Could they help? He began to be concerned about her, she had said goodbye to him in Dunedin over the phone. What did she mean by that? Was there a hidden message in her call that he had missed? He decided he must travel by night to be alert and on guard against the forces of darkness who would be at their strongest then. He recovered his 'spiritual suit' from the tree and asked a nearby couple in a car if they would take him to Amberly. Understandably they refused.

He set off wandering aimlessly along the banks of the Avon River and began putting questions to the ducks still on the river. He came to believe three quacks were yes and four quacks were no and proceeded to take his directions from them. He passed a house with lights still on and asked the ducks if he should approach it; they quacked yes.

The occupants invited him in and gave him food and coffee. They had a rather bizarre Salvador Dali print on the wall. He asked them about it but must have received a suitable reply. He was given a bed for the night but repeatedly woke up in a sweat, his mind a racing, swirling, tangle of confusion. He read sections from several books, looking for something, anything, to point the way out of this living nightmare other than suicide.

The Boy looked out the window, and, standing in the breaking light, was a monk-like figure in a long dark brown cowled robe, so loose fitting he couldn't make out a face underneath the hood. It moved slowly towards him across the lawn. The robe was made of a rough sack-like material so coarse he could see the weave. There was no walking motion; it glided through the early morning mist rising off the Avon River and, as it approached, it raised its left arm, and if he could have seen the hand in the shadow of the folds he was sure it would have been pointing directly at him. He screamed a silent scream of total horror as it dissolved in front of him. In the past he had hallucinated from fatigue, he had hallucinated from drugs, but this was no hallucination. There was no doubt in his mind that, whatever it was and whatever realm it was from, it was real.

He concealed the books he had been reading in his bag and left that amazingly accommodating couple, refusing their offer of breakfast, but noticing a written description of himself by the telephone. Who were they? Had he fallen into a trap? They were closing in quickly, he must get away. He walked into the central city to the Christchurch Cathedral, asked to see the Bishop to sort out his turmoil. The Bishop was busy so he approached the Curate and asked permission to climb the bell tower with the secret intention of jumping off. A group of bell ringers were practising their craft so he postponed his death.

He wandered the city with his bag, stopped in at a public toilet, took out his shaving razor and nicked his arm, mopping up the blood with sections of toilet paper. He mixed the blood with saliva and strands of his hair and proceeded to drop these 'markers' in various places around Christchurch, even managing to drop some in the tray of a couple of ute's stopped at the lights. His thinking was that if they were tracking him by means of his personal vibrations then he was going to make it as difficult for them as possible. The books he had 'borrowed' could also be a means of tracking him, so he stashed these in different spots around town.

He returned to the Cathedral and saw the Bishop, speaking to him rather cryptically as he did not know if he could be trusted. The Bishop suggested he travel to Jerusalem, not very practical advice at the time. So he decided there was only one solution and made his way up the bell tower as far as he could and out on to a small balcony. He paused to pray and, gripping the rail, began to swing his leg up. As he did so, a man in an overlooking office block directly opposite, fixed him in his gaze, picked up a phone and began dialling. My God, he thought, suddenly panicking, they have people everywhere; they will send someone to pick up my body, repair it and finish taking it over at their leisure. He must not let this happen. His death must be in secret.

What of his mother, he thought? He had drawn their attention to her by being in Christchurch. If they were tracking him so closely they must also be tracking her. What had he done? He had visions of her being taken over and her soul being lost to eternity as her body was converted to 'their' use. He could not leave her to this fate.

11 The Final Act

He made his way back down the tower, pausing every now and then to spin around clockwise on the spot as the tower steps turned to the left when descending, so, in his mind, generating 'negative forces'.

He rang his mother in Amberly. She told him that her boyfriend was travelling there on a soon-to-depart bus, and that if he intercepted it at a stop, then he could pay The Boy's fare. The intercept went as planned, and as the bus travelled to Amberly, The Boy noticed the driver wave at a passing patrol car. He was obviously part of their network and they were closing in.

They arrived and had a light meal. Was it drugged by the boyfriend? Which side was he on? The Boy watched television with them, he receiving 'messages' from it faster than he could process them. He went to bed. He had been given a bed in the same room as his mother; he didn't question why. Perhaps it was due to some form of propriety around his mother's and her boyfriend's unwed relationship or perhaps his mother felt responsible for her son's clearly unwell condition. Either way, he experienced a fitful night, tossing, turning and sweating profusely.

The next day, all three went shopping in Christchurch, The Boy trapped in his world of delusion, mind racing, verging on hallucinating with colours being very intense and the outlines of objects having a shimmering appearance, messages and double meanings streaming at him unceasingly.

An interesting but slightly disturbing ability accompanied this state. He found he was able to see auras. He had read of them in his occult books but now knew it was real. All organic objects, including people, had an energy field surrounding them. It varied in its intensity and colour. He could walk down the supermarket isles and see the 'life force' of items for sale. In one isle he was intrigued to see that unpolished brown rice had the strongest aura followed by white rice and then the packets of rice flakes had the barest of glows about them.

As they got back in the van, his mother passed him a comb and suggested he tidy his hair. As he did so, the comb crackled, proof that he was positive and the comb negative! Ironically, this was grounded in reality. On the way home they called in on someone, his mother's boyfriend talking quietly aside to them. The Boy was obviously the subject of conversation as he received a number of odd pointed looks from them.

As they completed the drive home, the boyfriend proudly mentioned that the roof of the Transit van had been relined. Was this to screen out positive solar radiation? Or to guard against tracking by the forces of darkness? They unpacked the groceries and carried them upstairs, The Boy performing his necessary right hand pirouettes while unobserved.

The next day was Christmas Day, which had become enormously significant to The Boy as he hoped Jesus, God, someone, something, would rain down on him and purge this evil from him and those around him. He woke early, prayed, and was disappointed that nothing had happened, nothing had changed. He turned to look at his mother in the bed beside his. She was lying on her back, sleeping silhouetted against the soft dawning light. He watched in horror as her stomach began swelling and continued until it almost touched the ceiling. It took on a darkness that wasn't so much a lack of light, but more a presence of blackness, so black that it appeared to be a void, a hole in space; she had become a portal to the other side he thought. It also symbolised to him that she was pregnant with unspeakable evil and it became clear that it was his duty as her son and the one who had brought this situation upon her, clear that he was now responsible for her, that he must save her from this fate which was taking her over.

He woke her and asked her to pray with him and to take off her wedding ring as 'they' would be using it to zero in on her. She complied. Again nothing happened; he decided he must take her life to save her from the fate that he knew was awaiting them both. Sobbing loudly as he did so, he placed his arm around her neck and rendered her unconscious.

Reaching into his toilet bag he removed the blade from his safety razor and proceeded to slit his mother's throat. He then slit his own and pleaded with his now fully conscious mother to lie on the floor with him and bleed to death. She refused, and he could not understand why. Her boyfriend, who had been sleeping in the other room, had woken from the noise and tried to overpower The Boy with a blow to the back of his neck. When he got to his feet his mother was gone. In his mind she had been taken by 'them'.

He pounded on, and yelled through the now locked bedroom door, "Mum, I'm sorry I've failed you," as in his deluded mind he had failed to rescue her from 'them', and therefore she was now fated to serve Satan and the forces of evil.

There were sirens and commotion and people rushing and shouting. His mother was taken away by ambulance. He lay on the bedroom floor tensing all his muscles, lifting his chin up and stretching open his throat wound. Blood sprayed in pulses all over the walls, speeding the emptying of his veins. As his blood and his life ebbed from him, he became lightheaded and a further sense of unreality crept over him. He lay down on the bed in deep despair over his failure and waited for death to overtake him.

A constable entered the room and sat in a chair, he guessed on guard, until other officers arrived. The Boy began raving about Satan and the evil they were supporting in taking his mother. He coughed to clear the blood in his throat and raised his head to clear his breathing, exposing the gaping wound in his throat where he had completely severed his windpipe. The constable turned instantly pale and dashed saucer-eyed out of the room to summon a second ambulance.

The Boy was placed in the second ambulance, still raving, this time about receiving intravenous saline solution, claiming that it was incompatible with his blood type and that the ambulance men were trying to make him negative when he was positive!

While in hospital he was under 24 hour guard. He still had not grasped the seriousness of his actions, still viewing them through his delusional construct, which justified all he had thought and done, and thinking that if only other people were able to perceive what was going on the way he did, then they would obviously understand.

The surgeon examined his throat wound under the watchful eye of a police officer.

"I used internal stitches on your trachea," he explained, "and external to close your skin. You are a lucky boy. It took eight pints of blood to refill your arteries."

When he had healed form his surgery sufficiently to be moved, he was transported to Sunnyside Psychiatric Hospital. There followed a seemingly endless succession of experts interviewing him and diligently writing pages of notes to be duly presented to the courts.

Following one of his monthly court appearances, where he was once again found not fit to plead, he was held in police cells and then transported to Addington Prison. This was done in error and against the instructions of the Medical Superintendent and the advice of the Senior Clinical Psychologist of Sunnyside. The Boy was still in a psychotic state, which consisted of periods of extremely heightened senses, floating on a baseline of terror. Owing to this state, he believed he had been, with the complicity of all parties, i.e. Carrington Hospital staff, the judge, the police, prison staff and inmates, brought to the jail to be killed. The Boy lay on his bunk warily watching the five inmates in the cell with him, wondering who would be the first to strike, what method they would employ and when the attack would take place.

As night fell, prison staff arrived and called him out. This is it, he thought. They placed him in a single cell where he spent the night occasionally drifting off to sleep, only to snap awake at any loud sound, the terror only diminishing as the sun came up and the prison day began. He was taken back to court that day and then back to Sunnyside hospital, still believing he had narrowly escaped death and not knowing who behind the scenes had orchestrated events.

He had received no medication during this time, and Sunnyside Hospital staff did not know what had happened to him, or even where he was.

He received an apology from the medical superintendant, but was still very fearful, not knowing whom, if anyone, he could trust. In fact he thought that she, the superintendant, was 'in on the plot', such was his mental state. The gravity of his actions still had not penetrated his reality. In one of his pre-trial interviews he told the psychiatrist that he expected to be in Lake Alice for six months or so.

During each of his monthly court appearances, The Boy was found 'unfit to plead' and remanded once again to the hospital. Slowly, each month, piece by piece, his delusional construct crumbled and the horrific truth of what he had actually done broke through into clear, inescapable realisation. What followed were periodic waves of intolerable guilt, anguish and uncontrollable sobbing, as the truth slowly leaked and seeped into his understanding and occupied more and more of his waking world.

Later, in May, when they thought him fit to appear, he was brought to trial, and after a court hearing followed by a jury deliberation of less than four minutes, he was found 'Not guilty on account of insanity' and formally committed to Sunnyside Psychiatric Hospital to be detained 'At Her Majesty's pleasure'.

ORDER FOR DETENTION OF PERSON AQUITTED ON ACCOUNT OF INSANITY

Section 39(g) (i) Criminal Justice Act, 1954
 To every Constable and to the Superintendent of the Sunnyside Hospital.
 ALAN GORDON MACKIE of Dunedin, Freezing worker was this day on his trial on indictment for Attempted Murder acquitted on account of his insanity.

The Court made an order that he be detained in a hospital within the meaning of Part V (a) of the Criminal Justice Act, 1954 as a special patient under the Mental Health Act, 1969.

This is to direct you the said Constables to take the said ALAN GORDON MACKIE and to deliver him to the Sunnyside Hospital and you the said Superintendent to receive him into your custody for detention in accordance with the order.

Dated this 9th day of May 1975 at the Supreme Court at Christchurch.

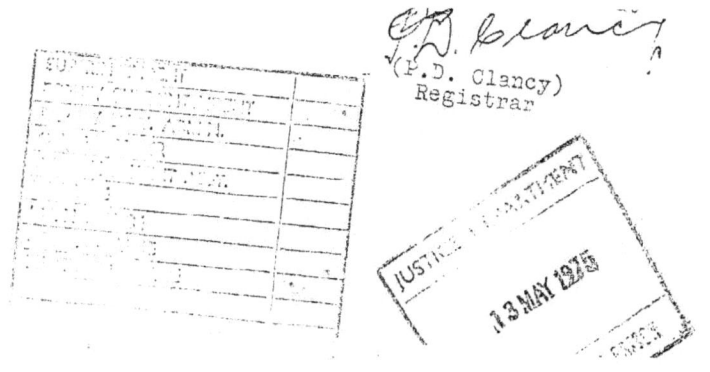

12 Desolation

Sunnyside, such a cheerful name for a psychiatric hospital he thought as he was driven back with his usual escort of nurses following his final court appearance. It was quite a pleasant setting on the outskirts of Christchurch. Leafy trees lined the driveways and broad lawns, with footpaths winding through them between generously spaced single story villas, the one original remaining brick and masonry building lending the only institutional-air to an otherwise park-like layout.

That was it; he was now committed to the institution. He had asked his lawyer how he should plead in court as it was all still a confusing barrage of words and procedures, people and places. He had given up his need to try to control what was happening to him as events moved at times with glacial slowness, then all was haste and flurry, then back to waiting. This had been the pattern for the last five months since he had tried to take his and his mother's life. Adding to his sense of unreality was the feeling that his body was out of synch with his mind, a situation he was still having difficulty with. He was being injected with a massive dose of the anti-psychotic drug, Chlorpromazine, every four hours around the clock. It slowed his mind a little and mitigated the fearful panic, which had been his waking state for perhaps a year now. This disconnect he felt between mind and body, however, was a fair price to pay for the reduction of the terror, which would previously and frequently wash over him.

He settled into hospital routine as best he could and began the long and difficult road back to sanity.

The Boy had never known such total desolation. It overtook and consumed everything. Each morning he woke up and experienced it all over again, as the understanding that his whole concept of what was true and what was not dissolved and evaporated around him. The guilt and shame bowed his head and drove his eyes downward.

He had always thought a little humbling is good for the soul, but this was crippling, even if nothing less was deserved. For the first six months of his hospitalisation he barely spoke. Such was the depth of his depression, that he felt anything he might have said was so trivial, so inconsequential and meaningless as not to be worth uttering.

It amazed him what conversations he became privy to when in this state, as those around him became used to his non-responsiveness and so, to them, he simply faded into the furniture. His frequent and greatest expression was when he burst into deep uncontrollable sobbing; it seemed to rise from depths within, stretching back to childhood, and carried a flood of un-cried tears from years past.

He had been committed to Stewart Villa, the general purpose admissions and semi-secure villa. It was a random assemblage of patients for whom they did not have purpose-built villas. It held people on remand from the courts for psychiatric reports as had been his case.

It also held patients who needed a degree of containment and control not available in the other villas. These covered the spectrum, from sexual offenders whose movements required close monitoring to one patient in particular who was the closest thing he had ever encountered to an animal in human form, from her appearance to her gait, which was an awkward stiff rolling motion, lacking any fluidity. It reminded him of a chimpanzee walking upright. Her intellect was such that she was incapable of language. She had had all her teeth removed because of her propensity to bite. The last straw had been when she bit a piece of ear off a baby who had been proffered to her by an unwise visitor. She was medicated to such an extent that she required regular enemas administered against her will by less than enthusiastic staff. The Boy and all others passed by her with caution.

She had a male equivalent, again without the power of normal speech, but he was able to utter short phrases in a very quiet voice. As with her, he had a fixed routine, which staff deviated from at their peril. He would lash out with ferocity at the source of any perceived tormenting. Luckily, he was not able to move without a staff member holding his hand and walking him very slowly. He had the less than endearing habit of relishing his farts, which were surprisingly frequent. He would raise himself off his seat, always to the left, with one elbow on the armrest and the other arm straightened, he would release his gas then lower his body back down with a very proud and satisfied grin on his face.

Another distressed and distressing patient suffered from Huntington's chorea, a slow degeneration of the central nervous system. This disease shuts down all the body's systems, starting from the more high level functioning system, subtle and refined, and progressing until the inability to breathe brings death. Along with other sympathetic patients, The

Boy found it horrible to watch. This patient also was at the stage of being unable to speak and her movements were a drunken lurching. She had difficulty swallowing and frequently coughed food and fluids back up, but it was her rage which was the most frightening. She was physically large and was, in addition, overweight. If her coordination had been intact, she could have inflicted severe damage. He did not know whether the anger was a reaction to her condition or a part of it. But it was fearsome to behold.

The rest of the inmates comprised a selection of the intellectually impaired, depressives, maniacal, and schizophrenics of varying degrees, as well as a sprinkling of those that an impatient and intolerant society rejected, or those who found society too fast, demanding and complex to navigate.

The Boy encountered the first person other than himself who held a fixed delusion, and, through that encounter, gained an objective understanding of the strength of self deception and the illogical nature of the phenomena. This patient was convinced that he was the reincarnation of Sir Isaac Newton. He had screeds of intricate mathematical calculations, all very complex, all with accompanying labyrinthine commentary and, to him, proving his claim beyond doubt. No amount of logical argument or evidence to the contrary would shake his conviction, which was, after all, mused The Boy, one definition of a delusion.

The staff also spanned a range of personalities and abilities. Some were warm and genuinely caring and worked hard to make the patients' stay in the hospital as comfortable as possible. Others found the prospect of immediate and unquestionable authority over a whole ward full of patients very appealing and exercised that power with quiet glee.

Some staff members were not the sharpest of intellects and coped with that in differing ways. Some with grace, humility and acceptance of their limitations; others would display their insecurity through brusqueness, intimidation, or the unnecessary exercise of their power. In contrast, one senior staff member completed cryptic crosswords with relative ease, enough in itself, but all the more impressive given English was not her native language.

Another older male nurse spoke thirteen languages, taught calculus at the local university and represented the region in chess tournaments. But his human relationship skills were abysmal and, when on evening shift, which was his preferred duty, he would arrive in his usual dishevelled state, the uniform clean but rumpled, his hair defiantly choosing its own course in life, giving the impression that it would have preferred not to be attached to this particular head. He would pull up a single chair to the chrome legged and Formica topped table at the end of the communal lounge. Carefully relocating the other chairs, he'd pull out his pack of playing cards and proceed to play patience, occasionally barking in a distracted manner, his eyes glaring both over his heavy rimmed glasses and out from under the veranda of his wild eyebrows at anyone who disrupted his routine. A routine which continued until it was time for him to go off duty. The Boy had tried on several occasions to engage him in conversation, but the unmistakable signals were that he would rather not talk; it seemed he found people bothersome at best, if not just plain annoying.

The student staff on practicum placement from the local university stood out clearly. They were usually young, mostly females, wide-eyed and apprehensive as they sat in their crisp new uniforms, overly alert, gingerly waiting for a patient to do something 'mad'. The braver ones ventured to engage with the inmates and obtain material for their current assignments, rather than just glean it from the text books, case histories and nursing notes.

The hospital routine ground on and was as exciting as the decor of plywood panelled walls and corridors, vinyl floors and tired vinyl-covered chairs and couches with their chrome tubing, heavy and awkward to shift, and somehow just the wrong shape to be comfortable. If one dozed off in a medication-induced doze, the tendency to slide down in the chair brought wakefulness jolting painfully back, if only temporarily.

The unrelenting cheeriness of the occupational therapist and other staff did its best to bring some stimulation to the inmates, with morning exercises and various activities slotted through the day – music, quizzes and arts and crafts, walks through the grounds, and the sparkling highlight of walking to the hospital canteen at the pace of the slowest patient, to spend a meagre ration of pocket money.

Now at least, The Boy was out of hospital pyjamas and dressing gown, which was the regulation attire for new admissions to the ward and which made them very conspicuous should they wander out of their designated area. Over also, was the locking of the door to the single room, which all and each had in common.

The first time he was escorted to his room and handed a large plastic bowl as a toilet, the heavy wooden door swung snugly closed and the key rattled noisily in the lock, the thick brass tongue with its hollow metallic clunk slotted home into the keeper of the door jam. All came as a cold shock, reminding him clearly and without ambiguity that he was not fit to be among human society, that he must be separated and caged. At that time, it still had not percolated through to his 'present' thinking exactly how his actions that had lead him to that place and time were perceived by others. He had discerned no malice behind the attack on his mother and naively assumed others would understand that.

His mind was very far from healed, still deeply damaged, his paranoid panic periodically rising unbidden, and clutched it's icy fingers around his heart and mind. At these times he believed once again that everything, including the hospital, was a farce, an elaborate facade, constructed, staffed and populated to convince he and a selected few that all they believed was false, but, in fact, hid the evil truth that everything he and others like him had stumbled upon was the actual reality. Then slowly, painfully, those vain imaginings would dissolve like snow under the spring rain of reason as he again adjusted to the crushing guilt, remorse and shame … until next time.

He could conceive no end to this cycle of despair and desolation.

13 Beware of Greeks ...

There remained for The Boy, the strong sense of another presence dwelling in him, manifesting itself at odd times in odd ways. On one occasion, as he sat in the lounge awaiting the next activity in the day's routine, he idly glanced over at a patient resting on a couch, both arms outstretched along the backrest. As he gazed, he thought he was seeing the line of the couch through the upper chest of the young man who had become semi-transparent. Doubting his eyes, he leaned forward, staring hard, trying to focus the 'illusion' away, only to become aware of the buttoned pattern of the couch also visible through the body of the patient. Needless to say, he mentioned this to no one, fearing an increase in his medication.

Another time, he sat with a pack of cards, casually flicking through them killing time, then, for no apparent reason, he began dealing them face down into two piles. When he had finished the pack he turned them over and found one stack wholly red, the other black.

During this period of his hospital stay, he was experiencing déjà vu several times a day. This troubled him, until he analysed the events that he appeared to have pre-knowledge of and found no value in the content. He came to the conclusion that there was nothing mystical or magical about the phenomena, that it was merely the result of a severely stressed and drug-damaged brain. The 'wiring' was disrupted and normal visual or aural input was somehow tracking through and firing off that part of the brain associated with recall, and as a result, what he was experiencing in real time simply felt like a memory.

He had no reassuring explanation, however, for a very clear and precise phrase he heard one day in perfect androgynous stereo, right inside his head. He was aimlessly knocking pool balls around the table in an empty games room when a voice said, "Put that down, that's not your game." He spun around in surprise, but apart from him, the room was empty. Again he thought better than to report this occurrence.

Some patients heard a one-sided conversation, although there was a heavily medicated patient who wandered about, loudly arguing with and berating the internal voices she heard. She clearly suffered under the barrage of abuse and directives that she experienced. He hoped that was not his future.

Happily, he never heard from his voice again. It was around this time that his ability to read people completely deserted him. This lack married up with his paranoia, and made some conversations virtually impossible. His thinking process, if he could call it that, instead of being linear and logical, had come to resemble a tree in form – the initial thought corresponding to the trunk – then quickly dividing into limbs of opposing thoughts and dividing again and again into smaller and smaller branches of contradicting possibilities, until he was left paralysed with a thousand runaway twigs forming a canopy of confusion.

For instance, someone may enter the room and say, "Hi!" He found he could not respond as his mind was avalanched with an ever expanding range of permutations. Did they mean they were high? Did they mean he was high? Did they mean they were high and shouldn't be? He was and shouldn't be? They weren't and should be? He wasn't and should be? Were they issuing an invitation to get high? Or were they just saying hello?

He simply could not decide and so was frozen into silence. These strange phenomena, save the last one, building on such pre-hospital encounters as the apparitions, the auras, the names at the party, the lunch orders incident, the playing cards etc abilities, which he knew were not of him, troubled him and carried with them the distinct impression that they were gifts. It was an inner knowing, an unspoken conversation, real estate rental. It was payment to him in return for him accommodating the presences within.

This interpretation was strengthened when he discovered the definition of the word genius derived from the belief that extraordinary abilities were attributed to a spirit or 'genie' accompanying the bearer of that title. A notion he had no difficulty accepting.

Weeks turned into months which turned into years. The days were sprinkled with incidents, one major one being where the hospital superintendent, who was also chief of clinical staff in Stewart Villa and therefore attended the Monday morning ward meetings in the day room, announced that she had been informed that The Boy had been seen both boarding a bus and also that he had been receiving LSD through the mail.

Neither of these allegations was true. However, he incurred loss of privileges and was once again confined to the dayroom and required to remain in pyjamas, a seemingly mild penalty, but with hospital life as crushingly boring as it was, it piled stress upon stress. His objections to this injustice were answered with a threat that if he did not quietly comply he could always be transferred to Lake Alice.

The mention of this institution already instilled fear in patients. News was just breaking about the use of Electro Convulsive Therapy (E.C.T.) inflicted as a punishment upon the child patients there. E.C.T. was routinely administered with electrodes applied to either side of the heads of patients. The electric shock seemed to have the effect of erasing recently laid down thought patterns and memories, and any depression stemming from these. So, erase them, erase the depression. This was usually performed under anaesthesia and a muscle relaxant as the severe muscular contractions had been known to break bones.

Unfortunately, one psychiatrist had taken it upon himself to administer E.C.T. to terrified children on their bodies and legs without anaesthetic, purely as punishment for what he had decided were incidents of misbehaviour. Such is the nature of unchallenged authority. Revelations of this were to break nationally and lead to an enquiry, resulting in dismissals and payments of compensation to the victims.

So threats of transfer to Lake Alice were used by some staff as a means of intimidation and control. These threats proved to be prophetic.

In time and duly cowed, The Boy had his

privileges restored and his boundaries extended. This was not to last.

A blatant abuse of power occurred one quiet afternoon following lunch when The Boy was seated with others in the wide corridor. The peace was broken by the distressed crying and wailing of a female patient as she was dragged by her ankles, on her back, along the floor by two male staff members, past the stunned observers. Her skirt was up over her head and her underwear exposed. This was a tiny woman, weighing no more than eighty pounds at most. She was also severely crippled and despite corrective footwear, walked with a pronounced limp. The charge nurse strolled in front swinging his bunch of keys in a triumphant and cavalier manner.

The Boy challenged the treatment saying, "There is no need for that!" and to "Treat her with some respect!" The charge nurse's face reddened in anger and The Boy was told to change into pyjamas and report to the dayroom. He protested and stated he had done no wrong in coming to the defence of a helpless female patient. Shortly after that he was confronted by half a dozen staff members who manhandled him to a bare room with a plastic covered mattress on the floor, held him down and injected him with chlorpromazine and haloperidol, the first being a broad spectrum anti-psychotic and tranquiliser, the second, it was later privately confided, was used to punish 'non-compliant' patients and 'to teach them a lesson'.

Through his painful and drugged state, he heard the next shift come on duty, heard a shuffling and murmuring outside his door, then a key rattled in the lock and it swung open. A particularly nasty charge nurse stood there with a group of staff who all advanced into the room. He was again held down, his nightshirt hauled up and the injections repeated. The Boy protested that he had already been drugged. The charge nurse replied with a leer that, "If it's not in the notes, then it never happened."

This treatment was inflicted several more times over three days of solitary confinement. The effect was to render The Boy continuously groggy, and caused severe pain in all his muscles and joints, which he was to describe as feeling as though he had received a kicking. When his punishment was over and he was released from the room, it required two staff to walk him to the showers. And true to the staff member's word, no mention appeared in the notes, save a sanitised version attributing events to his 'paranoid delusions'.

14 Moving

It came to pass that The Boy was summoned to the office and instructed that he was to be transferred to Cherry Farm, another saccharine name for a psychiatric hospital, this one serving Dunedin. The health department, he was told, had a policy of repatriating patients to their home towns when practical and it was now practical. His meagre belongings were assembled, they did not consist of much, as everything he owned had been picked up from the flat by his brothers and kept, sold, given away or destroyed. No record of him remained, right down to photographs. He no longer existed, he had been expunged from the family memory.

That final deletion was simply the formalisation of a process that had been clear that day in his bedroom when his family had lined up in united denial to his revelation of their parents' near separation all those years ago.

He was transferred, which may have spared him further abuse as he was told he had been shortlisted to receive what they termed 'deep sleep therapy'. This comprised patients being drugged unconscious for days and weeks on end, and only briefly revived during this period to be fed, showered and toileted. The thinking was that the enforced rest would allow the disturbed mind to heal itself. Reports later emerged in other hospitals of these comatose patients being routinely raped.

In his new setting, his privileges and paroles were gradually extended as he proved his trustworthiness. He sensed nothing unusual when a fellow Cherry Farm patient, without those paroles, asked him to purchase a bottle of aftershave from the canteen on the hospital grounds. He did so and returned with the specifically requested Old Spice. The purchaser thrust the change roughly into his pocket and in one smooth movement broke the top off the glass bottle on a convenient projection and swallowed the contents. The Boy stood shocked at the extent to which someone could be so totally owned by alcohol and noted to himself that he had better not perform that particular favour again.

Life in Cherry Farm slipped into a quiet routine that was not to last. His mother became aware that he was now living on the outskirts of Dunedin and, still fearing for her safety, demanded that the hospital transfer him. The Boy once again felt the sharp sting of rejection, but understood and accepted his mother's fear, and mourned his inability to assure her that, although he was still a very damaged person, the thinking which had driven his actions was no longer present, replaced instead by remorse, sadness and shame. He resolved to do his best to explain to her, his brothers and his friends, that the madness which had held his mind captive and led him to commit such an act was gone, and in doing so, he prayed he may receive a measure of forgiveness.

Consequently, he began writing an account of his journey into madness. This was kindly typed up by an administration staff member and he was able to post copies to his mother and two brothers. He received no reply.

He found himself on a plane to the North Island and then by road to the town of Marton and the infamous Lake Alice. He was pleased and relieved to find that Lake Alice consisted of two very distinct and separate facilities. There was the fearsomely titled 'Lake Alice Maximum Security Villa for the Criminally Insane' referred to as M.S.V. or colloquially as 'The Block', and then there was the 'Open Side', built long before The Block, and consisting of the semi secure Villa 8, a female villa and an adolescent unit, all three staffed around the clock.

Lake Alice laundry and workshops

Maximum Security Villa for the Criminally Insane

In addition there was a number of smaller two storied detached units housing about fourteen patients each, only some of which were staffed, and then only during the day and early evening. The other buildings were offices, a large and quite modern recreation hall with a built-in canteen, a separate kitchen and dining hall, an occupational therapy building and, away on the far side of the large grounds, a set of workshops and laundry.

The M.S.V., a long low single story building, was situated on the far side of the grounds behind tall concrete posts arching inward, and spanned with mesh up to the point of curving, and then with an alarmed strand topped by rows of barbed wire. Needless to say, it was out of bounds to all open-side patients, not that any wished to venture near.

To The Boy, the building seemed to emanate a presence, a crouching menacing presence, probably based as much on reputation as reality.

He was admitted into Villa 8, the semi secure unit, and settled into dormitory life. The lower floor was divided into office space, toilets, two lounge/day rooms, the larger one having a television and pool table, the smaller reserved for quieter conversation, reading and card games. Any other forms of table games didn't seem to last long as pieces or counters disappeared, making them unusable.

Life there was fairly austere especially for a

smoker, as pocket money for all patients was one dollar per week. The canteen was subsidised to such an extent that one dollar could buy a packet of loose tobacco, a box of matches and a packet of rolling papers. Along with many fellow smokers, The Boy kept a plastic bag in his pocket and all his butts were carefully allowed to go out, never stubbed, the charred strands of tobacco gently rolled out of the end and the 'roach' deposited in the plastic bag. Next payday, the contents of the new tobacco packet were teased out to spread over a Formica table top and the collection of rank-smelling butts opened one by one, the paper discarded and the inch of tar-coated tobacco sprinkled over the fresh ration, thereby increasing the entire stash by some twenty five percent, a significant amount to a nicotine addict and well worth the time taken, despite the evil smelling result.

In time, The Boy was first allowed to attend the occupational therapy department and found great delight in exercising his creativity with macramé, weaving, and then, joy of joys, he was permitted to attend the woodworking room. Under the tutelage of a somewhat eccentric instructor, he learned to carve and learned other skills. The instructor had some fairly unconventional views, believed in reincarnation, and routinely took instruction from whom he referred to as his spirit guides by means of divination with pendulums. After consulting them, he told The Boy that he was an old soul and had chosen the path of incarceration in order to learn spiritual lessons to take with him into the next life. The Boy listened, understood, but did not believe.

Owing to his apparent steadiness of mood and predictable behaviour, he was moved out to the semi supervised villas, to villa 15, which was staffed only during the day and early evening.

15   'The Block'

At this time, The Boy was on a twice daily 2mg. dose of Stellazine, an anti-psychotic, a minimal amount, but he still found it troublesome and had asked several times to be taken off it but was denied, as was his request to see a doctor so that he could put his request directly.

He eventually decided on direct action of a sort. He perfected the technique of flicking the small pill up alongside his upper gum with his tongue. With it in this position, he could comfortably drink water and show a supposedly empty mouth. To prove his point, which was that he did not need medication, he began to save up these pills in a plastic bag, which was hidden upstairs in the villa, suspended by a string, down the back of the hot water cylinder.

To build his case he periodically requested to be taken off the drug and also asked the staff member how he was doing behaviourally. He knew that every now and then these comments would make their way into the nursing notes. He knew this because he had managed to slip into the office unobserved and loosen the wing-top screw which fixed the fanlight window. When the staff had gone off shift for the night and the other patients were all in bed, he could quietly ease out the fanlight and reach through to open the larger window affording him entry. Then it was just a matter of uplifting his file and retreating to his room to read. Over time and using the notes as feedback, he was able to manipulate the entries made in his file.

He reached the point when he considered he had built up sufficient positive entries that he would risk a stand. Unfortunately, his cunning was not matched by wisdom, so when one day he decided to prove he did not need the medication by producing a bag bulging with some six hundred Stellazine tablets, he did not reckon on the degree of affronted pride and outrage this would engender.

The hospitals reaction was to send five burly staff members from the Maximum Security Villa, complete with hand cuffs, who bundled him into the transport van, taking him on what was a short trip, but a world away, to The Block. The van pulled up to the chain mesh and barbed wire gate, a male nurse standing on the other side, and after making eye contact with the driver, he unlocked the gate and swung it wide, locking the gate as soon as the van was inside. He then strode over to a nondescript door with a small very thick window in it and one of those Formica inscribed name plates which read LAUNDRY SERVICE ROOMS.

The van door was not opened until the nurse had unlocked this heavy wooden door and stood with one hand on the door knob, the other hand on the key still in the lock and attached to his belt with a metal chain. As The Boy was ushered into the building, he was confronted by a wall of floor to ceiling metal bars with a barred gate fitted in the middle. This divided the room in half, with another wooden door in the concrete block wall opposite, again with a thick glass viewing-slit mirroring the one they had entered through.

The outside door swung heavily closed and was locked by the guard who had opened it. The whole arrangement reminded him of a submarine airlock, providing a transition portal from one environment to another, and as far as freedom was concerned this performed a similar function.

The Boy was not to pass through that door again for a rather long time.

The wooden door leading further into the building swung open and one staff member walked in and locked the door behind him He strode forward and unlocked the metal gate dividing the room in two, all stepped through the gate, which was again locked, and only then was the wooden door leading into what he was later to learn was known as the south corridor, opened. He was marched into the corridor and stood in front of yet another heavy wooden door, fitted with the now familiar narrow slit of window with very thick glass. This door had a double skin, the second skin covering two heavy lengths of metal strapping, which rotated with a system of levers and slotted into metal keepers bolted into the concrete, providing four anchor points in addition to the deadbolt.

A square plastic bin was brought to his attention and he was directed to strip naked and place all his clothing in it. He was issued with a knee length night shirt of heavy cotton material, the door was opened, and he was told to step into his euphemistically termed 'bedroom'. It was completely bare save a plastic covered mattress on the floor, a woollen blanket, double stitched to prevent it being torn into strips, no sheets, no pillow, a plastic tumbler, a jug of water, a toilet roll and a plastic bucket. The concrete floor was covered with vinyl, the walls were painted concrete block, the ceiling made of painted concrete panels and the windows spanning the two metre wide room were of safety glass behind bars. Through this he could see a small dank exercise area with walls stretching up three metres to square mesh, framing a distant patch of sky. He was told tea would be brought to him and the door closed and locked.

Dinner arrived as did the next day's breakfast, after which he was escorted to the ablutions to shower. This routine continued for three days, during which time he began to hallucinate, an experience common to all inmates, as the brain, starved of stimulation, begins to create its own. After these three days, he was released into the main outside exercise area with the rest of the inmates, the area sufficient to contain a full sized tennis court with a strip around the perimeter.

In addition to this, there was a small covered section set into the wall, with a long concrete seat, and a radio for entertainment fixed high up on a shelf. The walls were about four meters high, and overlooking this 'yard' was a tall tower with sloping mirror-glass tinted windows, reminiscent of an air traffic control tower. One staff member was always posted in the tower when the inmates were in the yard and had constant radio communication with the control room, which monitored all movements via CCTV cameras, and in addition the tower had an open link to the local military base.

The Block, when commissioned, was the most secure institution in the Southern Hemisphere, and at the time of The Boy's incarceration held fifty occupants, thirty of whom were there for capital offences.

So this is where you go if you don't take your medication, he thought, *or*, more seriously, *if you offend the ego of staff.* He later learned from reading the Act, that his transfer there was illegal, as prior permission must be obtained in writing from the Director General of Mental Health. In fact, quite a number of patients were 'ghost' inmates, mysteriously transferred back to the 'open side' of Lake Alice prior to the biannual visit undertaken by the Review Panel, a team of senior psychiatrists who periodically conducted a status review of patients who appeared before them for assessment.

The Medical Superintendent of Lake Alice used The Block as his personal holding pen for patients who upset the smooth running of his hospital and as a further reminder of his power. The Boy was placed on a regime of injections of medication every three weeks, the effect of which nearly killed him.

The first week following injections, he was reduced to deep depression and despair and spent much of his time sleeping, which was difficult. His mind was crying out for sleep, but the only opportunity for that was in the large chairs of the day room or on the concrete exercise yard, both of which were totally unsuitable. The second week of his three weekly drug cycle saw his despair lifting and he could bring himself to talk to fellow patients. The third week would find him joining in the outdoor volley ball or games of cards inside. Then would come his injection and he once again submerged within himself and sunk into the quicksand of depression.

This cycle was made all the worse by the knowledge of the injection's approaching inevitability. Any requests to have his medication reviewed were simply ignored. He dreaded it so much that he had planned his suicide. He had decided to run at full speed into the concrete wall at the end of the exercise yard, lowering his head at the last second and smearing his brains on the concrete. He had rehearsed it, chosen the spot and paced out the distance. It was only a friend who kept reminding him that the blackness would lift, that stopped him from carrying out his intentions.

Each inmate was allocated what was termed a 'special interest' nurse who spent time with them and to whom the inmate could turn for answers to difficulties they may be encountering. The Boy's special interest nurse was a huge Dutchman of high intelligence and steady wisdom. He had been in the field for a number of years and enquired if The Boy had an uncle of a particular name. He replied that he did not. A week or so passed and the nurse came back to him and informed him that indeed he did have such an uncle. This had been his father's brother and a chronic schizophrenic who had lived and died in Seacliff Psychiatric Hospital outside of Dunedin. The Boy was shocked to learn that his parents had never spoken of him; he felt a measure of identification with his madness and certainly with his ostracism. The cause of schizophrenia was, as always, still enmeshed in debate – is it environmental or genetic? No room was allowed for a spiritual component. As he lay in bed that night he pondered deeply on this and wept for a man he had never met, and vowed that, because of a potential genetic inheritance, he would never have children if such pain could be avoided.

There were moments for humour amongst the sadness, such as the time he saw the visiting GP for relief from the constipation caused by his medication. The doctor was very much old school with the high and lofty air derived from his clear superiority to the distasteful rabble he tended.

The Boy told him of his constipation from the medication; the doctor produced a foil-covered bullet-shaped suppository from the cupboard and said, "Now you know how to use these and that you are to remove the foil don't you?"

"Yes," replied The Boy.

"Good. I'll see you next week then," the doctor replied.

The following week The Boy was presented to the doctor who asked how the suppositories were working.

"I don't like them," said The Boy. "They taste terrible, and for all the good they do I might as well stick them up my backside!"

The doctor's eyes widened, his jaw dropped, his mouth opened then snapped shut into an angry slit as The Boy winked and he realised he had been played with. The nurse, who accompanied The Boy into the consultation room, had great difficulty not laughing as he quickly bustled him back to the yard.

The Block had an Occupational Therapy (OT) department consisting of two divisions, one strictly for woodwork and the other for craftwork in general, and catered for all disciplines from rug making and cane weaving through to what became The Boy's preference, leather carving. He gained such proficiency that the instructor commissioned personal work from him.

Time began to drag, the routine of the days stretched out ahead. In due course, the staff considered him sufficiently compliant, and forwarded his name to appear before the 'Review Panel', a gathering of august luminaries who determined the fate of all inmates, general committals, and 'special patients' as those held under section 39 were termed.

The Panel assembled every six months and reviewed the nursing notes, then interviewed patients placed before them by the staff of The Block. He was summoned and his responses to their questions must have satisfied them, as all medication was immediately stopped. However, life in The Block continued, the days stretched out into the future with no end in sight. The policy of the institution, and indeed the nature of mental illness itself, was that patients were never given any dates, but were told they would be released when they were 'well enough'. The months drifted slowly by.

16 There and Back ...

The single most debilitating and life altering event of The Boy's hospital stay occurred when, with very little warning, his life's possessions, consisting of a suitcase and a paper rubbish bag of assorted clothes and personal items, were gathered together. With his possessions and twenty dollars which he just happened to have, he was deposited in Cuba Mall, Wellington, a city he had never been in and in which he knew no-one, having previously lived all his life in the suburb of Abbotsford, Dunedin.

He saw a Salvation Army office in the Mall so he made his way there. It was closed so he waited until it opened. He introduced himself to the officer who found him a bed for the night in what was euphemistically described as a boarding house. The building was in Abel Smith Street, it was two storied, unlocked and unlockable, in filthy condition, with rubbish littering the interior. It had a communal kitchen, a toilet and single rooms, all in semi-derelict condition with graffiti on some walls, holes in the others, and unknown substances smeared about. The only other resident was an elderly Irish alcoholic who staggered about threatening and abusing both The Boy and any other person who wandered through, but, as it transpired, 'the others' had no business being there.

All of this was extremely disorienting considering the very quiet and controlled environment he had been in only a matter of hours before. Just crossing a road presented quite an obstacle. He had difficulty coming to terms with the degree of 'culture shock' he was experiencing, he had not cooked himself a meal, washed any laundry, coped with traffic or shopped for groceries in six years. No arrangements had been made by the hospital for contact, follow-up, support or monitoring. His 'rehabilitation' consisted of being wished-well as the car, which left him in a strange city, drove away.

With the help of the Salvation Army officer, The Boy began to come to terms with the situation he found himself in. The officer assisted in finding him a job as a kitchen hand at a Salvation Army owned hotel in Cuba Mall. The fellow tenant in Cuba Mall hotel had someone who visited regularly from Presbyterian Social Services. Basically, this person came in the morning as he knew he would find his charge in then, he would wipe the vomit off the wall, strip the old gentleman, get him in the shower and give him a fresh set of clothes and clean sheets. He'd bundle up the dirty clothes and sheet and take them with him, and repeat it all every couple of days.

One evening when the boy had returned from work, the alcoholic lodger staggered in, lurched through to the kitchen, and, producing a bottle from his coat pocket, he placed it heavily on the table. With a shake of his head he said, "Whoa this stuff is powerful!" giving it an out of focus, but wary and respectful eye. The boy looked at the label, 'Claytons' it read.

"It has no alcohol in it," said The Boy.

"What?" exclaimed the elderly lush. "I've been swindled!"

It took some time to convince the gentleman that some firm would go to the trouble of making something non-alcoholic, dress it up as alcohol and sell it in pubs. He finally understood and, no happier, weaved back down the corridor and out into the night, vowing vengeance.

The Boy stayed at the dish washing job until he found another job in Kilbernie managing a craft shop, but the pressures of coping and the constant aloneness he felt were too much for him. Depression descended with all its cold clawing darkness, until he knew he had to take action before he slipped into an irretrievable state. He turned to the one person he had some degree of trust in, the assigned psychologist at Lake Alice.

The Boy rang and told him that if he didn't receive help 'he would be swinging off the rafters inside a fortnight.'

The Boy was told to ring back in half an hour. He did so and reluctantly the hospital agreed to accept him back if he arranged his own transport from Wellington to Lake Alice. This he did whilst thinking they had found no difficulty in dropping him there! But he was desperately in need of help as he felt the ground was coming up to meet him, very quickly.

His return to Lake Alice was greeted with different reactions from different people. The Boy was not in the mood to respond appropriately to their greetings, it would be some time until the ego-crushing experiences of his attempted reintegration back into society and his consequent descent into the familiar black hole of depression faded, and his fragile personality showed itself over the parapet of his emotional fortress.

Most inmates welcomed him warmly; one notably different response was from the absent-minded paranoid patient who was always misplacing his shoes and complaining to staff that The Boy was responsible. An enthusiastic and physical response to his return was received from a young man who, from their first meeting, had 'taken a shine' to The Boy.

He was in Lake Alice as a result of his promiscuous behaviour, which would be aimed at anyone he felt attracted to. He was light on intellect and heavy on libido, but meant absolutely no harm, and would fondly hug and fondle the objects of his attention in a socially inappropriate and blatantly sexual manner but with no malice or thought of harm. He was an inmate more for his own safety than that of others. This young man was to prove instrumental in the life of The Boy, but that incident was not to occur for some months.

Life settled back into its stultifying routines, punctuated with unpleasant instances, one such instance being the time when his in-growing toenails became infected. He reported this, expecting a short course of antibiotics until the nails grew clear of the flesh and could be trimmed proud, which, from experience, was the best method of managing the condition. However the resident doctor took it into his head that he would remove them.

The Boy expressed as much dismay as he dared, but the climate was still one of fear and intimidation. He was spoken about as if he was not in the room and the course of action was decided. His toenails were removed, a very unpleasant experience involving local anesthetic, scissors, pliers and requiring some time in a wheel chair until they healed.

The toenails eventually grew back exactly as before, which he knew they would, as in-growing toenails are a genetic condition and not correctable by surgery. The doctor never enquired as to the results of his experiment.

The young psychologist he had phoned and who was fairly newly appointed to the hospital met with him and asked if he wanted to join a therapy group. He agreed. Anything to break the routine and add some interest was welcome. The group met a few times and then disbanded, but he maintained his contact with the psychologist who on one occasion quietly warned him to "Watch out," that he had enemies on the staff. "They don't like you," he said. "You threaten them. Not only are you physically strong but your intellect makes them feel insecure."

This enmity was played out when the regular charge nurse went on leave and was replaced by a nurse of very generous proportions. She was a cow of a woman and openly racist. She was also the one who had overseen his toenail removal. She doted on the Maori patients whom she referred to as "My boys". There was a small weekly ration of tobacco, papers and matches, which was used as reward payment for patients performing duties about the villa. She commandeered this and simply doled it out to 'her boys' in the security of autonomy.

During her tenure, The Boy developed a severe headache such as he had never experienced before. His requests to see a doctor or more senior staff member were blocked by her. The headache continued for weeks and was only attended to when the regular nurse returned from leave. Aware that it would not have been feigned, she organised a barium sulphate scan at the Base Hospital. This revealed nothing as the pain had eased just days before the test was administered. The Boy suspected a spiritual element to the event but of course could not mention this.

Another occasion featured the same abusive nurse. He had been troubled by the flaring up of a cyst at the base of his spine and had it excised at the Wanganui Base Hospital under general anaesthetic. When he awoke, he was immediately transported back to Lake Alice between two large staff members, but the discomfort from sitting over the transmission hump caused him to ask them to return to get a pillow. This was done, but the pain from the surgery and the nausea from the anaesthetic had him hovering on the edge of fainting for all of the forty mile drive.

He had been privy to the Wanganui hospital

doctor's strict instructions delivered to the transporting nurses about bed rest for a week, to only be up occasionally, then extending to mild exercise. This did not take into account the personality of the Maori charge nurse who, from day one, insisted that he be up and about and attend the dining hall for meals and occupational therapy during the day. His protestations of pain were dismissed and under her reign of fear and intimidation he was forced to comply.

It wasn't long until this activity caused the sutures to saw through the flesh of his buttocks and the wound to burst open. He showed the damage to his instructor at O.T. who immediately called the doctor. He was transferred back to Villa 8, with bed rest and daily flushing and dressing of the wound until it eventually closed.

He never received any form of apology regarding this but was privately comforted by junior staff members too afraid to speak out. It was said of Lake Alice staff that the good ones either changed for the worse or left.

17 ... And Back Again

This was when his friendship with the highly sexed young man changed the course of events. As he steadily healed from the splitting of his wound, he was transferred upstairs to the dormitory.

One evening, The Boy allowed an evening visit and chat from him to evolve into him sitting on the bed and his hand wandering under the bed sheets, whilst with his other hand he guided The Boy's onto his bulging pyjama pants. Unbeknownst to either, a patient, seeking favour from the staff, had quietly crept downstairs and reported the situation. In a very short time and equally quietly, the staff member stepped suddenly into the dim dormitory and shone his torch on the two.

As a result of this offending, it was decided The Boy would be returned to The Block. The young man was not punished as he was deemed to be at risk if sent there and, more significantly as it later transpired, he was the 'special friend' of a senior male staff member.

The softening up technique prior to his departure was to place him on what was termed 'suicide watch'. It was actually a punishment. The patient determined to be at risk of suiciding was stripped naked and locked in a room furnished with a bucket as a toilet, no toilet paper as "you could kill yourself by choking on it", a plastic jug of water, a double stitched coarse woolen blanket and a plastic covered mattress.

It proved impossible to sleep with his bare skin against either the heavy plastic or the prickling of the coarse wool. The best he could manage was a little rest by lying on the bare vinyl floor against the wall with the mattress tented over him and the blanket rolled up and used as a pillow. The result, as intended, was a rather compliant, sleep-deprived patient. The 'suicide watch' was a sick joke as no patient was checked on during the course of a very long night and, if anything, pushed toward rather than away from any self destructive feelings.

He slotted back into the pace of The Block with its steady and predictable rosters and routines. Life there, as on the open side, was rife with homosexual activity, although of necessity the activity in The Block was more clandestine.

The Boy was not without 'friendships'. This

conflicted him, as increasingly he did not want to have these thoughts and feelings, but seemed irresistibly drawn to them. There were sad aspects to these relationships. A young man whom he considered to be his best friend and with whom his contact had grown through attraction to a more healthy respect and caring, was being bribed with cigarettes by a staff member into providing oral sex.

This happened under the noses of the other staff members. The patients were allowed into the toilets only on the hour and the half hour, the toilets being locked in between those times, although the staff let themselves in and out at anytime. This particular staff member was extremely obese, and under cover of his immense girth, The Boy's friend would slip into the toilets ahead of him, perform his service, and then slip out behind the emerging nurse.

Bedtimes were in three shifts and, if on full privileges, one could choose which shift to retire on: six, nine or eleven o'clock. On occasions, this same staff member would escort the early patients to their cells and once they were securely locked in for the night, return to his victim's room, and under the pretense of counselling him, stand with the door ajar, shielded from the surveillance cameras, and claim what he had paid for. The Boy never reported this as to do so would result in the punishment of his friend. Besides, he did not trust 'the system' to act properly.

He had in the past complained to the Ombudsman regarding his illegal transfer to The Block, and of the fact that he had not been allowed to access his own copy of the Mental Health Act, only to find himself confronted with a note from the Ombudsman's office with his letter attached. He realised with a sinking feeling that The Ombudsman's office had chosen not to reply to him, but merely referred his letter straight back to the hospital superintendent.

He discovered later that the hospital had a policy of opening all mail, both incoming and outgoing, and not telling either patients or the senders of the incoming mail that they were vetting all correspondence and, if they so chose, would not pass it on, either inserting it in the patient's, file or consigning it to the rubbish bin. All this compounded the feeling of being isolated from the outside world, of helplessness, and of both being at the total mercy of others and the pointlessness of appealing any situation.

He began to sink back into the deepening darkness within, which, month by month and year by year, was claiming evermore of his heart and mind.

One day, with the aid of his friend, he took inventory of his fellow inmates. His friend had cut the penis off a young boy with a pocket knife, resulting in his death. This disclosure shocked The Boy to the degree that he never got around to asking what the motive for such an extreme action was, but then again, he himself had slit his own mother's throat and still found it difficult to explain his state of mind at the time, which was his only justification. As The Boy and his friend looked around the dayroom, they identified another man who had cut the penis off a boy, this time with the edge of a tobacco tin. One patient had beaten his mother to death with a cricket bat, another had chopped up an acquaintance with a spade for spilling beer on his stereo, another took great pride in recounting how he had stabbed someone forty two times. The Boy suspected this very macho stance was masking some fragile emotions.

As their gaze travelled the room, it took in a huge Maori man, the proverbial gentle giant, who had murdered two policemen by simply beating them to death with his bare hands, another who had shot two policemen and was always a gentleman in many senses of the term; he spoke softly, was very polite and respectful, he read books on philosophy and enjoyed classical music.

As was the unwritten custom, The Boy did not enquire of any fellow inmates the motivation for their actions or, indeed, even the reason for their incarceration.

The Block's contingent ranged widely, and included an inmate of obvious diminished intellect who had raped a three month old baby, through to a fully qualified clinical psychologist who had sexually assaulted a young child patient. All in all, of the current compliment of fifty two inmates, thirty were in for capital offences. The Boy saw and understood that this was where he deserved to be, this was where his actions had led him, he was amongst his peers.

This acceptance of his rightful status deepened and solidified his depression. It reached the stage where he again decided to end his life. He felt he could not stand to sink any deeper than he already had and so the time had come to take the final step.

18   I Balanced All

One of the crafts practised in the O.T. department was printing in the traditional way with individual lead letters assembled by hand in a printers block. The spacers were of various thicknesses, right down to thin strips of lead shim which had a striking resemblance to the blade of a craft knife.

At the end of each OT session, all tools and implements were placed on a shadow board or in specific holders, right down to the needles used to hand-stitch moccasins, and all had to be accounted for prior to the inmates being counted out of OT and back into the corridor. So a strip of lead shim, cut to size with one edge carefully shaved, was substituted for the blade of the craft knife and hung boldly in its place on the shadow board, the real blade slipped down the spine of a book and smuggled out of OT. The Boy told no one of his decision and that evening went off to his room with the book and the blade.

He waited until the staff had completed their last evening rounds and the room lights were switched off, leaving the longest possible time before he would be discovered. He removed the blade from its hiding place and began to focus his mind.

> *I balanced all,*
> *brought all to mind,*
> *the years to come seemed waste of breath,*
> *a waste of breath, the years behind,*
> *in balance with this life,*
> *this death.*
>
> ©William Buster Yeats.

All his faults and failings paraded through his mind. A river of pain and misery stretching back as far as he could remember. His depressed mind expertly filtered out any times of happiness and contentment and left him thinking only that he had brought nothing good to anyone, nor to himself. He could not think of anything to live for, all was bleakness and despair. He was of no use to anyone, no one wanted him, especially his family. He would be doing the world a favour in removing himself from it. His family would no longer be burdened and shamed by his existence. It all made perfect if painful sense. These were his thoughts as, in the moonlight angling through the barred window, he ran his finger along the razor sharp edge of the craft knife blade.

But underneath these feelings ran another voice. No. Voice was not the right word, it was quieter, but nor was it a whisper, it was a gentle current, one that was drawing him, one that his mind could not swim against. No, that was not it either; it was more that he did not want to swim against it. It was a warm welcoming current. A current that had a presence, which softly but irresistibly compelled him to slide out of bed and onto his knees.

He found himself saying out loud, *"If this is God, if You are real I need You now, please take over the wheel, I'm not fit to drive."* With that he found himself instantly deluged under an immense waterfall of what he could only think of as love. It poured over, around and through him. It confounded his ability to put into words what he was experiencing because he had never experienced anything like it before. But that did not matter, it was not a time for words. It bypassed and surpassed his intellect as he was washed by wave after wave of forgiveness, acceptance, and a cleansing healing peace, both externally and internally that could have only one source. He didn't just think, he now knew, in the deepest part of him that God was real, He did exist, and further, that he was loved and accepted by Him despite every reason not to be.

The waves continued. His unspoken but internal protestations that he was not deserving went unheeded, he did not know for how long. Time had been suspended, it ceased to exist, he had to ask for the outpouring to stop, he simply could not take anymore. He climbed back into bed and fell into a deep sleep knowing life had changed forever; nothing would be the same again. Now he knew that hole in his heart had been filled, that constant ache was assuaged, he knew deeper than knowing that he was loved.

19 Where to?

The next morning he could not stop smiling. He surrendered the craft knife blade to a nurse, blurting out a garbled account of his experience of the night before.

He should have known; confessing that caper earned him a return to the South Corridor, three days of solitary confinement, a mattress on the floor, and a six o'clock bedtime. And so back to the bottom rung of the privileges ladder he went, but quite frankly he didn't care. He now had something no one could take from him. When he emerged from solitary, and for the rest of the week, other patients were puzzled by his irrepressibly good mood to the point where some asked what drugs he was on and could they get any.

One day he was visited by an old flatmate from Dunedin who had become a Christian, and his wife. The Boy lamented his continued time in The Block, and asked rhetorically when he would get out. His friend mentioned another mutual friend who also had become a Christian, whom, he said, had a spiritual gift he termed *'Word of Knowledge'*. This gift, he explained, was the ability to put a question then pass on the answer received, he believed, direct from God.

"I'll ask him," his friend said.

The Boy was a little sceptical, however, given his recent encounter, was open to anything. A short time later a letter arrived and the 'word' was he would get out when he accepted that he may never get out. *Fat lot of good that is,* thought The Boy, and sunk back into the endless routine. His continued detainment in The Block was unjustified in his mind and rankled, finally reaching the point where he decided that was it, he had given up. 'The System' had institutionalised him, so 'The System' could look after him for the rest of his life.

He had barely had time to settle into this new mode of thinking when, without warning as was the policy, he was whisked out of The Security Block and over to the 'Open side'. Only then did his friend's *'Word of Knowledge'* come back to mind.

Once again, routine became his life, then with little prior notice, he was told he was being transferred to Auckland to a place called Carrington Hospital.

So, off to the airport and up to Auckland.

Carrington was a very different hospital from the others, although his initial placement was unpleasant. It was a behaviour modification ward, structured around a system of rewards and punishments where he once found himself receiving demerit points for not contributing sufficiently to a mixed gender group discussion on menstruation.

This stay was thankfully short, his behaviour was assessed as not requiring modifying, and he was soon transferred to a large open ward with a wide range of patients and positive upbeat staff who emanated an attitude of respect toward the patients, which was refreshing and sadly lacking in the other establishments. It had the effect of making the inmates want to live up to the staff's expectations of them.

The information slowly trickled out to him that his release on to the streets of Wellington by Lake Alice Hospital had been the subject of much discussion, finger pointing and internal disciplining of staff, as there had been zero planning or follow up. This was news to him and being told of it at the time would have gone a long way toward easing his profound sense of personal failing. Happily, the sink or swim school of rehabilitation was not a model used in Carrington as he was soon to discover.

They had, on the grounds, a couple of former staff accommodation houses, which were now used as group homes whereby three or four patients were selected to live together in the house. They were set up with sickness benefits, which they had to arrange to have paid into their own bank accounts, and from this money, they paid rent to the hospital and bought their own groceries, cooked their own meals, and essentially lived in a flatting situation whilst attending the usual hospital groups and activities.

This was exactly what The Boy needed, a supported and steady transition from the long years since his breakdown, his years of incarceration and total dependence, to a gentle transition back to living in society. He began, in increments, to regain the confidence which his mental breakdown had totally shattered, and to regain the courage and the fragile hope that just maybe he could make it on the 'outside'.

He had the cheery assistance of a resident psychologist whom he saw on an infrequent basis. Although, again, he had to a degree, filter the information he shared with her as any incursion into spiritual matters saw her shut down and retreat to an attitude of caring but paternalistic superiority, as, in her opinion, these ideas of his were clearly those of a delusional mind. An interesting departure to this stance was allowed, however, when The Boy let slip that he could 'dowse' or 'divine' water. He had been reading a book on the subject, such was the continuing hold of fringe areas of knowledge on his mind.

He experimented with 'rods' made from cotton reels and bent wires. He found he could easily locate underground pipes and demonstrated this to the psychologist. She was most impressed, as was he, especially when he thought he had made a mistake in the line of a pipe and repeated the trial, only to find himself consistently erring at the same spot, only to later discover that the underground pipe took a sharp bend at that very point. He continued his reading but abandoned it when the authors spoke of divining at a distance using maps and also across time, making it obvious that he was not dealing with natural physical forces but supernatural ones. It was another 'gift' which he had to eschew on his long slow climb back toward God.

Despite most of the staff being respectful and caring, there still remained the odd example of former times. The staff all of course had full access to The Boy's nursing notes, psychiatric assessments, and reports of his interviews with doctors over the years, and some took advantage of it, with one staff member often catching him at isolated times and sexually propositioning him, on one occasion taking The Boy's hand and thrusting it down his pants and onto his very large erect penis.

Another staff member boasted of being given a ten

year old boy for the night, on his fortieth birthday. As this was close to the age when The Boy had been re-seduced, he found it particularly distressing, but based on his previous experience with the ombudsman's office, felt it pointless to report it.

There were other incidents, minor in themselves, but the scales often tipped against him, as with no contact from family or relatives and being some distance from friends in Dunedin, he was isolated and an easy target for any staff member so inclined.

One day, owing to toothache, The Boy made an appointment to have a tooth looked at by the hospital dentist who elected to pull it. He was a little fearful as the dentist appeared slightly drunk, but this puzzled him as he could smell nothing on his breath, so rather than make a fuss, after all it was him or no-one and he was in pain, The Boy said nothing. The dentist proceeded to inject his gums and extract the tooth, the process was clumsy and very painful, he finished and dismissed The Boy, who returned to the group house on the hospital grounds where he lived with three other patients.

Later that night as the anesthetic wore off and the pain grew, his tongue located several pieces of broken tooth in his gum which were attached and several which were not but had been driven into the gum. The unattached ones he removed with a small pair of pliers. The pain settled a little, but he found that every time he swallowed, the attached pieces tugged and bled. As this was now the early hours of the morning, he removed these with the pliers, cut a strip of cloth as a plug, and walked down to the staffed hospital ward to obtain some pain tablets.

The next morning he was seen by another hospital doctor who expressed professionally-contained alarm at the excavation. The Boy was placed on prescription pain medication. The dentist soon 'retired'. The Boy received no apology, but took comfort in the fact that no other patients would be made to suffer by that dentist.

20 Come out of the Man

The Dunedin friend who had visited him in The Block was now living in Auckland. He, along with his wife, had temporarily moved there so that he could attend Bible College. During the course of The Boy's stay in the transition house, his friend picked him up and took him to a 'home group' meeting. This was a mid-week gathering of Christians for prayer, worship and 'ministering' to those wishing it. It was held in the house of the son of a prominent Christian evangelist. The son himself was an emerging leader in the Christian world.

The Boy went along with a high level of nervous anticipation, feeling all sorts of swirling emotions. He was no stranger to these feelings and was in a state of alert ambivalence. He knew the power of evil and had experienced its ability to deceive and overpower his mental defences and invade his mind. As they drove to the meeting, he could sense the gathering spiritual forces, like a silent whirlwind spinning and churning. He knew by the strength of the 'storm' that this was going to be a significant evening.

The meeting opened with prayer and moved into song. The Boy had never heard such beautiful singing before and was transported to realms he had never visited. His LSD experiences had come close, but always had a taint of artificiality about them that was totally absent here. This place he was in carried an assurance of absolute safety, purity and solid sanity and that unmistakable presence of love he was developing a hunger for. He felt held and protected.

As the evening progressed, the offer was extended and he went forward for prayer. He stood between the evangelist's son and his prayer partner. They placed their hands gently on his shoulders, closed their eyes and assumed an attitude of listening. Then, as one, they both opened their eyes, turned toward one another and he spoke to her saying, "There is a spirit of murder here."

"I agree," she replied.

With that they began to pray in 'tongues' and the 'storm', which had fallen away with the singing, began again in earnest. The room retreated until The Boy felt himself standing seemingly alone in the storm's silent roar, he could feel the gentle but firm hands on his shoulders and hear the 'tongues, swirling about him, but it was as though he was in a distant place, far removed from that affluent Auckland suburb. It could have been a snow-lashed Himalayan mountain peak or a lonely Saharan sand storm, such was the sense of separation in time and place from the lounge room of the 'home group' and the total immersion in a tumultuous spiritual battle.

Through the maelstrom he heard a clear voice, this time in English, asking him, if he chose to do so, to repeat the following words as he was led in a statement of his confession of sin, his intention to turn from that sin and his desire for Christ to be his Saviour. As he went to speak the words, he found his mouth was not under his control, his mind was clear but his lips were locked shut and refused to form the words; the battle was on. He had no mental ambiguity about following the prayer, but his mouth simply would not work. Then, slowly, struggling intently, syllable by syllable, he managed to voice his desire, and word by word the opposition lessened.

The ministering helper then commanded the 'spirit of murder' to leave The Boy in the name of Jesus. He felt a physical jerk as something departed his body and disappeared straight through the wall in front of him. He did not see it go with his natural eyes, but there was no doubt in his mind that that was where it went. There was also no doubt that this was the entity that had pierced his fragile defences and taken up taunting residence within him on that long distant day on a Dunedin beach.

He went home that night, knowing that he was one major step closer to where he wanted to be, but also knowing that he had strayed so far from God that it was going to be a very long road back.

The time came when it was decided to move the group of rehabilitating patients from the Carrington Hospital house on the grounds into the halfway house the hospital owned. It was a large villa-style residence in Dominion Road, which had been bequeathed to the hospital board by the former owner, a doctor.

The group tentatively but gratefully moved in. They were a struggling bunch of misfits, all with shortcomings and failings, but none-the-less all strove to work together to get along and find their stumbling way in the world. Some at various times found work, The Boy included, although he also at times fell back into despair and depression, and once again had to retreat to the safety net of the sickness benefit. He was still in the subtle but firm grip of marijuana and tried, though not too hard, to shake it off. Whatever income level he found himself on there always seemed to be a way to eke out enough for a joint or two.

He decided to obtain his heavy traffic licence and did so by offering his services free of charge to be an off-sider to the truck driver at a local timber company in return for the driver giving him lessons in driving. The firm agreed to this and in a short while he obtained his licence. Using this new qualification, he gained a period of work delivering for a large small-goods wholesaler.

It was during this period of his life that he acquired a dog. One of the flat mates had a female dog, which fell pregnant and The Boy kept one of her pups. This dog was responsible for an immense amount of healing as he discovered that the animal's ability to give unconditional love allowed him to drop the wall around his heart, just a little.

He well understood the story within the Pink Floyd album *'The Wall'*, as the central character of that themed work retreats under a succession of insults visited upon his psyche, and brick by brick builds a wall to shield himself from the hurtful world he inhabits, only to find that in building a wall of protection, he has also successfully constructed a prison, one which he must now work to deconstruct, brick by painful brick.

The Boy was also handicapped by the fact that when he began his serious exploration of the world of drugs, his emotional, social and psychological growth ceased at that point, thereby leaving a boy in a man's body. He now had the task of reintegrating his fractured and fragmented soul, striving to make up the many years of maturing which his peers had long ago negotiated, leaving him trailing far behind.

His multiple demons had not entirely deserted him and several mornings whilst walking to another job at an assembly factory, he found himself sobbing aloud and was thankful that no one saw. He did not recognise it as depression, merely assuming it was his lot and his place. He did not yet have the insight or knowledge that the nature of depression carries with it the feeling that it will never end, the conviction that the sufferer will always feel this way.

His past still reached out to hold him in other ways as well. He sat one day and sketched one of his flatmates, the drawing formed off the end of his pencil with ease and virtually drew itself. It was very accurate but immensely unflattering, it was a caricature of the woman, highlighting and exaggerating all her negative features. He had never experienced this facility before and previously had worked quite hard to produce even a passable likeness of anybody. The result scared him as again he knew it was not a skill he owned and was one more he knew he would have to surrender.

The same skill manifested itself again, this time in a small wooden carving of a face intended to be worn as a pendent. He formed it with a vegetable knife, again with consummate ease. It had a distinct and troubling presence and he was quietly thankful when a girl, one of the stream of flatmates, 'acquired' it from him during a brief but quite pleasing physical relationship.

There was a steady parade of colourful characters who spent varying amounts of time in the half-way house. They were voted in and occasionally out by the group as a whole.

His encounters with the supernatural world still came and went, mostly when least expected, as on one occasion when he was walking into Auckland city with a friend. They had smoked a joint on the top of Mt. Eden but, as with other times, he knew this joint did not cause the following vision, but proved to be a catalyst in parting the veil between the two worlds.

His friend was extremely intelligent, but lacked a measure of 'street smarts'. The Boy saw the threat one hundred yards off, as a 'skinhead', moving with the arrogant measured swagger perfected by the French Foreign Legion, sauntered toward them. The Boy manoeuvred himself between his friend and the approaching thug, gently shepherding him to the edge of the footpath. As the hood came closer with his shaved head, multiple tattoos, muscle shirt, braces, tight black jeans and Doc Martin boots, The Boy could see quite clearly his dominant demon. It was as if it was being projected onto his face and stood out about an inch in front of it, not quite in synch', and moved a fraction out of time with its host. It had very coarse hairy skin and a pig-like snout, but what struck him most was the penetrating red eyes.

The Boy fixed his own eyes on it, with his best 'I see you, and you don't scare me' look. This look was returned with a puzzled and unsettled fear flickering over the red orbs as the entity realised it was visible to this particular human. Thankfully, they passed without incident.

The Boy was still struggling with his addictions and had reached a point where he decided that he needed to take action to break free of them or be dragged under. The half-way house was working well; there was a very functional roster system operating that The Boy had borrowed from a university student flat he had often visited in Dunedin. It consisted of two concentric circles of card, the larger outer fixed one was sectioned up around its rim with the chores requiring rostering and the smaller inner disc was mounted on top with the names of the flatmates around its rim. This was advanced clockwise one 'chore' each week ensuring a fair division of work.

He signed forms to discontinue his responsibility for gas and electricity at the half-way house. He made enquiries about a residential rehab' he had heard of, operated by a community of Christian families on Great Barrier Island, only to find it had closed and the families had all moved together to another town.

He followed up the directions given and tracked them down to a collectively owned camping ground. He decided he needed to join the group to help him climb out of the hole he was sliding into, so said his goodbyes to the current residents of the Dominion Road half-way house.

YOU LORD

You Lord are all I have,
and you Lord are all that I need.
To you Lord I give all I am,
for you Lord, to guide and to lead.

I give you my hopes and my dreams,
I give you my plans and my schemes,
I lay them all at your feet,
for you are my drink and my meat.

I give my first and my last,
I give you my future and past.

I give you my life and my breath,
I give you my life and my breath.

You Lord are all that I have,
and you Lord are all that I need.
To you Lord I give all I am,
for you Lord, to guide and to lead.
       Alan G. Mackie 2006

21 Onward and Downward

A friend had contacted him in recent weeks and asked if he could help him run a half-way house he was setting up in Coromandel Town. He agreed, and putting the Christian community on temporary hold, he, his dog and possessions, set off south.

The Boy was once again on a sickness benefit. It had become the pattern of his life and one which caused him a deep sense of guilt and shame in being dependent on the taxpayer. He worked when he could, but he seemed unable to maintain that level of stability and concentrated effort for any length of time, and soon slipped into increased depression, anxiety and insomnia, until he once again had to hang his head, resign his job and seek the understanding of a GP. When his friend asked him to help run a half-way house, he figured it was pretty much what he had been doing already, so why not give it a crack? He hadn't counted on the mental condition of his friend, who, as it turned out, was a manic depressive and whom he had previously only seen when he was in his stable phase between extremes.

Over the following couple of months, this combination of two strong but fragile personalities proved a volatile mix, and, under the pressure, he suffered a mild psychotic episode with his paranoia flaring up to the extent where he asked to be driven through to the local hospital and tranquilised until he regained his weak grip on reality.

The Boy decided to use this cross-road to make the move to the Christian community, only to find they had disbanded and gone their separate ways. He figured this town was as good as any, so applied for a job, found accommodation, and he and his dog took up residence. Little did he suspect that he would not leave there for the next thirty years, thirty years of alternately working and not working, periods when he was back on the sickness benefit, periods of successful self employment, periods when he slipped back into drug use. Times when he strove to gain God's favour, times when all he could do was fall into his Saviour's arms and plead his mercy.

He was very much still finding his feet in the spiritual sense. He was attending the local Christian church and discovering that the ability he always seemed to have, that of being aware of the non-physical realm, had been in a sense, sanctified. It was as if it had been surrendered, reconditioned and returned. It popped up at unexpected times. He discovered it even had a name, 'discernment of spirits'. On one occasion, a young lady asked him to pray for her as she wanted to give up smoking. He protested that he himself was a smoker but she insisted, and so he began.

As he stood beside her seat, laid his hand on her shoulder and commenced to pray, his mind was impressed with a clear picture of a rampant horse rearing majestically, mane tossing, but still, frozen. He dismissed the image and continued to pray but it returned. He mentally apologised to God for his wandering attention and resumed prayer. The horse returned. He realised it was being deliberately brought to his attention.

He addressed the girl. "Do you have a picture or a statue or anything, of a black horse rearing up on its hind legs?"

The girl thought for a moment. "No," she said. "Nothing like that."

"It's just that I keep seeing this picture of one in my mind," said The Boy. "If you figure out what that might mean, let me know, O.K.?" he said.

She agreed and he put the matter out of his mind. Later that evening as he was going to sleep he asked again what that vision meant. The reply was immediate. 'Look at your tobacco' were the words that came to mind. He did so and there clearly was a rampant horse as part of the brand logo.

At that time, The Boy was cleaning the local supermarket to bring in extra money, so the following night he went straight to the tobacco carousel, took a sample from each stack and laid them out on the counter and one after one, somewhere among the shields and crowns, scrolls and swirls, a number of the packs featured a horse. The Boy pondered on this and came to the conclusion, right or wrong, that just as the god Baal of Biblical notoriety chose to be worshipped in the form of a bull, so the dominant spiritual entity behind that company chose to be acknowledged in the form of a horse.

Another time the supernatural leaked into the natural was when he was working as a cleaner in a hotel from eleven p.m. through to six a.m. With a whining vacuum cleaner strapped on his back and therefore no welcome distraction of a radio or television, he was left alone with just his thoughts and was shocked at the content of the internal dialogue which streamed through his mind. It was a barrage of negativity, not in an audible voice, but it might as well have been, it was just as single-minded, forceful and clear.

Thoughts such as … "Look at you, you are a

waste of space, you are a pile of shit, you always have been and you always will be … Why don't you kill yourself, why bother living? … The world would be better off without you."

He realised he was in serious trouble and that he would not be able to stand long under this demonic deluge. He turned to the one place he felt he could gain help, the church. This was to prove to be a mixed blessing. The resident pastor was an elderly man of deep wisdom who carried a strong anointing and whose prayers God honoured. The Boy grew a lot in spiritual strength, knowledge and in personal healing.

On one notable occasion, a visiting church speaker was available at a 'shared lunch' held after the Sunday service in the house of a church elder. The Boy asked him for prayer; the minister stood beside the seated subject, laid hands on his shoulder and became lost in earnest prayer. A succession of Scottish heraldic shields or coats of arms sped past The Boy's closed eyes like roadside signs on a midnight highway. This made no sense to him save to set the stage.

The area being brought to his attention was clearly to do with his Highland heritage. The shields faded and he saw a huge man dressed in rough workman-like clothing, but looking distinctly Scottish with red hair, a thick beard and the ubiquitous kilt.

He held another more slightly built countryman with his left hand by bunched cloth at his throat. As The Boy watched this farmland scene, the burly Scot, with his right hand, grabbed the other around the crotch and, lifting him horizontally above his head, paused, then drove downward and skewered him straight through the spine on a narrow fencepost.

The Boy, glad there was no sound accompanying this vision, saw flesh, bone and blood explode through the stomach of the unfortunate victim. The Boy knew he had just witnessed an ancient and gruesome murder.

He rapidly retreated to the garden outside the peaceful country house peopled with pleasantly smiling chatting churchgoers, nibbling politely on their asparagus rolls and sipping tea. He was left with the clear knowledge that this act of violent killing was in his family history. He spent several days in periodic contemplation and prayer for forgiveness from the victim's descendents and for the damage done. In time he felt the stain lifted, the grieving gone, and perhaps a curse broken.

A similar vision in terms of gravity was when an acquaintance asked for prayer. So The Boy gathered his thoughts, quietened his mind and began to pray. He was immediately struck by an ancient and powerful presence around his friend. As he allowed the impressions to coalesce and begin to firm, he saw a gathering of robed figures in a thickly wooded area.

He asked the seated man, "Are you aware of any connection with Druids in your ancestry?"

"I don't know," the man said. "But I do know one of my relatives in the Catholic Church sold indulgences."

"No, it's not that," The Boy replied.

As he spoke, the cloaked figures in the wood became clearer and his viewpoint changed so he could see a bound figure suspended by his feet on a long rope from a tree limb high above the group. He was spinning faster and faster as the tightly twisted rope unwound. The Boy watched with growing horror as it became clear this unfortunate individual was being sacrificed. He had been suspended upside down for so long that blood was rupturing out of ears, eyes, mouth and nose, and spraying out on the upturned ecstatic faces and open mouths of the gathered circle.

The Boy reeled to another chair in the room and sat heavily, waiting until the nausea from what he had seen faded. He sought internal counsel as to whether he should share this experience, then waited some more time before he was able to tell his friend what he had prayed against in his forebears.

This habit the 'other world' had of popping into his

world had its pleasant side, also. One of those was when he suddenly had the confident knowledge that one of the congregation was pregnant, so he took quiet delight in gently advising her that.

"Oh, by the way you're pregnant … and it's a boy!"

"No, I'm not!" she said, smiling wryly at what she thought was more mischievous fun from The Boy. But, in due course …

Unfortunately the elderly incumbent minister retired and passed his mantle on. Under the new leadership, The Boy was told that since he did not speak in 'tongues' this was proof that he was not 'saved' and therefore was bound for hell. It took him a long time to come to terms with this new, more powerful and far deeper form of rejection, but then eventually he fully and confidently understood that his Bible did not support that view.

His Bible said that when he received Christ, Christ himself would send the Holy Spirit and the Spirit would decide which spiritual gifts to bestow and in fact listed the gift of 'tongues' as the least in importance. In addition, he found deeply personal matters he sought prayer for with the elders of the church had found their way into discussion among other groups. It was also reported back to him, that, owing to his having been in a psychiatric institution, he could not really expect to have any position in the church.

It was with huge regret and after many hours of soul searching, prayer and weeping, that he stopped going to that church, knowing he was mentally, emotionally and spiritually in a safer place away from it.

The years passed by, mostly uneventfully. Then there came a time when the whole world it seemed, was talking about child sexual abuse. The Roman Catholic Church, among others, was in upheaval over the abuses committed by priests, principally on young boys. It was on the television and the radio, and in the newspapers. If The Boy was with company when a news item came on, he quickly had to find something to do in another room. If he was alone, he simply burst into uncontrollable gut-wrenching sobbing. He had finally reached the place where he knew and had to accept that his repeated childhood rape and years of prolonged sexual violation was the cause of his life-long struggles. This was the volcano that rumbled beneath the surface of his life, continually unbalancing him and defeating all his attempts to stand firm.

He also knew that it was beyond his personal power to quell this Vesuvius; he had exhausted all his resources, he had run out of supplicating rocks to roll into its gaping maw and he had worn out all the platitudes. He knew he needed expert help.

The Road to Recovery diagram.
The multiple symbolism is as follows:
The Boy is depicted as naked and barefoot.
Above him is the unreachable 'highway of life'.
One arm is shackled.
The knife in his back reads church.
The crutch is named drugs and alcohol.
The leg irons are attached to the ball and chain of 'childhood sexual abuse'.
The tumbling rocks are variously:
    'Be a man!'
    'Get a job!'
    'Bludger!'
The fence palings are:
    'I've told you what to do a thousand times',
    'Stop looking for sympathy',
    'God helps those who help themselves',
    'Just get on with your life',
    'You need to fill in these forms',
    'Some people you just can't help',
    'You don't fit the criteria',
    'Stop dwelling in the past',
'   You don't qualify for assistance'.
The track dropping towards him requires another to descend it, bridge the gap, chainsaw down the fence and administer first aid.

The road to recovery

22 Out the Other Side

The Boy sought help from the psychiatric wing of the public hospital and they in turn referred him to a nearby clinic. He pressed the doctor there about counselling for his past abuse. He was determined not to be fobbed off again as had been the case during his sojourn through the government institutions. There, every time he had tentatively raised the subject as he had during all the endless encounters with psychiatrists, psychologists, doctors, counsellors, nurses, every one of them had either ignored, dismissed or minimised his distress. This time he was not going to let it go.

The doctor gave him a phone number to ring; it was for The Accident Compensation Corporation (A.C.C.), an organisation he was to have a great deal to do with over the coming years, some of it good, most not so good. They sent him a list of accredited counsellors. He had a brief but strict criteria. One, his counsellor had to be a Christian as no one else could possibly understand where he was coming from. Any other person hearing him speak truthfully of his experiences would simply refer him back to a psychiatrist, complete with their anti-psychotic drug cabinet. Number two requirement was that they be male, as the things he had to share he could not comfortably speak of with a woman.

There were only two names on that list that met his needs; one was in Coromandel Town, the other in Hamilton. He chose the Hamilton number and picked up the phone.

He was put through to the counsellor and found his voice had deserted him. The Boy finally stammered to the patient man at the end of the phone as the silence drew on, "I … I … can't speak."

"That's O.K.," replied the calm kind voice. "Take your time."

Through tears and an inability to make his mouth work, The Boy experienced afresh that evening of deliverance in the home of the evangelist. He eventually, with silent prayer, managed to state the reason for his calling and arranged an appointment.

Therein began a long and tortuous journey back to life, a life irrevocably rent at the age of three, a life that had taken a terrible turn all those years ago. He set out not knowing the length of the coming journey. Not knowing that he would have to re-visit that place of incalculable pain and walk hand in hand through the years with that wounded child, through all the events, all the abuse, the rejection, the despair, guiding and comforting the inner boy, reliving the experiences, walking side by side with that young soul and correcting the false understandings planted in his mind by those with vested interests and the twisted interpretations given to incidents and actions by those with evil intent; pausing here awhile with the young boy, to allow him to absorb the shock and take in at his own pace the immensity of what had happened. Resting there awhile to gather strength before tackling the next mountain or valley, the next hill or stream. Waiting, as the long lost child slowly understood through his adult eyes that what had happened to him was not his fault. That it had been done to him, not by him, planting and nurturing the hope that it was possible, after all, to reintegrate that shattered mind, that fragmented personality.

He steadily came into his own realisation that often what psychiatry calls psychosis is the mental clutch disengaging in order to protect the mind from a world that doesn't make sense. That what is labelled schizophrenia is the result of dissonance, of conflicting information and confusing thoughts and feelings, not the cause of them. It is the mind in overload, sometimes from spiritual attack, and therefore it follows that any psychotropic drug is treating the symptom and not the cause.

An astute mechanic knows sometimes it's the car, sometimes it's the driver and sometimes it's both. The Boy also knew as healing slowly percolated down through his being, that a wise and gifted counsellor had probably saved his life.

The following years proved a difficult road as he gradually found his feet and a new way of being in the world. He knew he would never be totally free from the abuse of his past. He often experienced what the therapist termed 'triggers', such as the time in a supermarket when a particular combination of talcum powder and perfume wafted down the checkout queue. He immediately felt a wave of panic, a terrible sense of being trapped and having to get away.

He stepped out of the line and, under the pretence of fetching a forgotten item, abandoned his shopping and hurried out of the store. At home, when finally he lifted his head from the tear dampened pillow and rolled onto his back, he was still not clear about this new trigger. It was too far back in his memory to be retrieved. He did know it was associated with the lady down the street. He remembered years ago from idle 'cup of tea' talk around the kitchen table that his mother had not, for whatever reason, breast-fed him. This service was taken up by the lady down the street. He also knew that he had a fear of that house. Exactly why, he would never know.

There were many of these triggers. Another example was when a friend gave him a leather belt he had outgrown. It was a very nice belt and he liked it a lot but had to give it away. The jingle the hasp and buckle made when loosened was exactly the same note as the belt buckle of his molester. In each case he did not know those memories were buried there, but there they were, waiting, just below the surface, like a snare laid under a thin covering of leaves, springing unexpectedly and sending him straight back to that time, that place, and the helplessness and fear he had felt back then.

He had learned what Post Traumatic Stress Disorder was, and he knew it would always be with him. The best he could do was manage it and trust that over time it would fade. Another long-term effect, as much from the drug taking as the abuse, was his delayed maturity. This, he hoped, would slowly catch up to his physical age and with time may eventually fall into synch'.

What he perceived as his biggest handicap, however, was his crippling vulnerability and sensitivity to rejection, and hinging on that, his inability to form and maintain intimate relationships.

He made a couple of half hearted attempts, but knew his fear of trusting or letting down his guard, would inevitably sabotage his efforts, so resigned himself to life alone.

He used his time to take up study and gained a certificate in Community Mental Health, then, finding therapeutic value in the exercise and taking heart from his small success, The Boy earned a Certificate in Social Services. Using that resilience-building educational venture as a long and gentle on-ramp, he merged onto the academic motorway, eventually exiting with a Bachelor Degree in Applied Social Sciences.

Postscript

Prior to publication of *The Boy*, Alan Mackie decided to give his manuscript to persons in his workplace as well as to a few trusted professional colleagues to read. He did this, knowing that it could damage his credibility as a safe, competent and professional social worker.

He died at the age of 60 on 26th of October, 2012, not knowing what the outcome would be – whether he would be accepted and respected for the person he had become or whether he would be stigmatised by his past and discriminated against, bringing to an end his future employment as a social worker.

He took the risk, because his ultimate goal was to tell his story so other survivors might find validation and understanding on their journey in search of truth, healing and freedom from their painful past. For this we honour Alan's courage.

Friends of Alan Mackie

The Boy with his uncle and father.

The car Alan bought from Governemnt funds, paid as compensation to patients for abusive treatment in the mental health institutions.

Alan gesturing his feelings on the steps of Carrington Hospital.

FINANCING AGENCY

2 April 2012

Mr Alan Mackie
C/- Cooper Legal,
Wellington
Private & Confidential

Dear Mr Mackie

Apology

You have a claim against the Crown Health Financing Agency (CHFA) seeking compensation for the suffering and distress you endured as a patient at Sunnyside and Lake Alice Hospitals. Your account of this period of your life indicates that the hospitals failed to take care of you in the way that you could have reasonably expected and for this I am deeply sorry.

The CHFA assumed responsibility for the actions of the former Area Health Boards and their predecessors as part of the Health Reforms in 1993. As such we acknowledge the serious allegations you have made in respect of the care you received while a patient.

Your experiences were clearly traumatic and I can only imagine how vulnerable you must have felt. This together with the ongoing effects your admission has had on your personal life is tragic and I offer my heartfelt apologies for all that you have had to endure.

CHFA considers that changes to legislation, training and models of care have assisted in making mental health services considerably safer for service users nowadays. And to this end I am encouraged that what you experienced should not be repeated today.

Whilst I recognise that no amount of compensation can put right what you had to endure, I genuinely hope that my acknowledgment of your claims and this apology will help you to bring some closure to these past experiences, give you a sense of peace and help you move forward positively with your life

Please accept my very best wishes for your future.

Yours sincerely
Crown Health Financing Agency

Alastair Scott
Chair

Level 2, Tourism & Travel House
79 Boulcott Street, Wellington
PO Box 5358, Lambton Quay
Ph 04 472 3310. Fax 04 472 3311
www.chfa.govt.nz

Social Workers Registration Board
Kāhui Whakamana Tauwhiro

CERTIFICATE OF REGISTRATION

This is to certify that

Alan Gordon Mackie

met the requirements for provisional registration as a

Registered Social Worker

on the 1st day of December 2011

Registrar

Dated this 12th day of December 2011

The above person is provisionally registered under s14(1) (a) having graduated after 1 August 2008 from a SWRB New Zealand recognised social work qualification. Provisional registration for graduates is valid for a period of two years from the date of completing the recognised qualification. Prior to the end of that time a competence assessment, as determined by the Board, must be completed to move to full registered.

Registration Number 4475

Social Workers Registration Act 2003

Important: A current practising certificate must be held by the above named practitioner to enable him/her to legally practise in New Zealand. The practising certificate will specify any restrictions or conditions that the above person's registration is subject to. The practising certificate must be made available to view on request.

newzealand.govt.nz

Alan G. Mackie
23rd March 2011
Bachelor of Applied Social Sciences

NAME		
MACKIE Alan Gordon		
BIRTH PLACE		
Dunedin New Zealand		
BIRTH DATE		SEX
6 March 1952		Male
HEIGHT	EYES	
1.74m	Brown	
DISTINGUISHING CHARACTERISTICS		
PASSPORT NUMBER	ISSUED AT	ON
A320500	AUCKLAND	13 AUG 1982
UNLESS RENEWED EXPIRES ON		13 AUG 1992

THIS PASSPORT IS VALID FOR ALL COUNTRIES

OFFICE AND DATE OF ISSUE

DEPARTMENT
OF INTERNAL AFFAIRS
13 AUG 1982
AUCKLAND

Poetry and Lyrics quoted in this book:
The Final Cut, Pink Floyd
Sing a Song of Sixpence, Alan Mackie
Hey Little Boy, Alan Mackie
Little Boys are Cheap Today, Alan Mackie
The Boy, Alan Mackie
Sleigh Me, Alan Mackie
Brain Damage, 1973 Pink Floyd
An Irish Airman Foresees His Death, William Buster Yeats

Suggested reading:
101 Frequently Asked Questions about Homosexuality by Mike Haley
A Child Called 'It' by Dave Pelzer
Experiencing Psychosis by Jim Geekie, Patti Randal, Debra Lampshire, John Read.
Leaping upon the Mountains by Mike Lew
Making Sense of Madness by John Read
Male Sexual Abuse Sequelae Chart on website. antonroest.co.nz.
Models of Madness by John Read
Rethinking Madness by Parris Williams
The Shack by William P. Young
This Present Darkness by Frank E. Peretti
Wild at Heart by John Eldridge

Contacts:

Accident Compensation Corporation 'Sensitive Claims Unit' 0800-735-566 www.survivor.org.nz (male survivor's website)

Doctors for Sexual Abuse Care,
P O Box 90723, Victoria Street West, Auckland 1142
Phone: 09 376 1422 Fax: 09 376 0790
Email: dsac@ihug.co.nz

Male Survivors of Sexual Abuse Trust MSSAT 0800-677-289

Patients' Rights Advocacy 64 07 8435837 www.PatientsRights.org.nz

www.ingramcontent.com/pod-product-compliance
Lightning Source LLC
LaVergne TN
LVHW051114080426
835510LV00018B/2028